Praise for *How Children Thrive*

"The real title should be *How Children (and Their Parents) Thrive*! Dr. Bertin's nonjudgmental and reassuring tone is the perfect antidote for the parenting book that makes us feel like we're doing everything wrong. Understanding a child's developmental capabilities at different ages and working to their strengths is worth the price of admission. And that's only chapter 1! I can't do my twins' first ten years over again, but now I'll go into their second decade MUCH more confident that I have the tools to handle what's ahead."
WENDY MASS
New York Times bestselling author
of *A Mango-Shaped Space*

"*How Children Thrive* is a breath of fresh air. Mark Bertin cuts through all the overwhelming theories on how to optimally raise children and presents an elegant, effective, yet simple approach that can help your child develop into the best version of themselves (while maintaining your sanity!). If you've ever felt overwhelmed as a parent, this book is a must-read!"
ELISHA GOLDSTEIN, PHD
founder of A Course in Mindful Living

"*How Children Thrive* is a book I highly recommend not only for parents but also for professionals who work with children and their families. Mark Bertin has done a masterful job of explaining the key role of executive function (EF) in a child's development and has offered very specific, practical suggestions for nurturing EF, self-discipline, and resilience in children. As Mark shares his insights about parenting, I was especially impressed with his ability to do so in an empathic manner. His warmth and humor as well as appreciation for the challenges parents face were evident throughout the book—making it easier for parents to understand, accept, and apply the information he conveys. This book is a wonderful resource for parents in developing self-compassion and resilience in their own lives so that they are better equipped to develop these same qualities in the lives of their children."
DR. ROBERT BROOKS
coauthor of *Raising a Self-Disciplined Child* and *The Power of Resilience*

HOW CHILDREN
THRIVE

Also by Mark Bertin

Mindful Parenting for ADHD

The Family ADHD Solution

Teaching Mindfulness Skills to Kids and Teens
(contributing author)

HOW CHILDREN
THRIVE

The Practical Science of Raising
Independent, Resilient, and Happy Kids

MARK BERTIN, MD

sounds true
BOULDER, COLORADO

Sounds True
Boulder, CO 80306

Published 2018

Cover design by Rachael Murray
Book design by Beth Skelley

Printed in Canada

Library of Congress Cataloging-in-Publication Data
Names: Bertin, Mark, (Psychologist) author.
Title: How children thrive : the practical science of raising independent,
    resilient, and happy kids / by Mark Bertin, MD.
Description: Boulder, CO : Sounds True, [2018] | Includes bibliographical
    references.
Identifiers: LCCN 2017040624 (print) | LCCN 2018003468 (ebook) |
    ISBN 9781683640219 (ebook) | ISBN 9781683640202 (pbk.)
Subjects: LCSH: Parenting. | Parent and child. | Resilience (Personality trait)
    in children. | Child psychology.
Classification: LCC HQ755.8 (ebook) | LCC HQ755.8 .B478 2018 (print) |
    DDC 306.874—dc23
LC record available at https://lccn.loc.gov/2017040624

10 9 8 7 6 5 4 3 2 1

With love and appreciation to my one wife,
two children, three parents, four grandparents,
and the rest of my extended family and friends

Contents

Foreword

I FIRST MET MARK BERTIN, MD, when he emailed me about a mindfulness group he was leading for parents out of his pediatrics practice in New York. We stayed in touch in the years after and finally met in person at the wonderful Mindfulness and Youth Conference in San Diego. What started as an email turned into handshake, then a weekend of swapping stories and science about child development, mindfulness, executive function, and more. I squeezed every moment out of the conference breaks to talk with him. Some evenings, we chatted late into the night, rattling off new inspirations and ideas about parenting, pediatrics, psychology, mindfulness, and more. That's because Mark is a guy with amazing ideas.

Since that time, I've been both honored and grateful to say that Mark Bertin has become a friend and collaborator. I've devoured and recommended his books to colleagues, friends, clients, and anyone else who will listen. But nothing has excited me more than this book you are holding in your hands right now in this very moment—one that every parent and child professional should have on hand in their office or on their nightstand, or maybe both.

How Children Thrive offers a scientific yet straightforward guide for raising thriving healthy and happy children. You will find pearls of wisdom on every page and down-to-earth, real-world advice for all manner of challenges that families face in the 21st century, from screen-time battles to social media madness. The irony is a lot of the advice you'll find in here may sound old-fashioned, and yet it still resonates for families today—and what's more, has solid research backing it up.

Too many of today's parenting books offer only trendy, simplistic opinions and theories masquerading as books. Not only do they rarely look at the research, they are often just one or two ideas that could fit into a few bullet points on a PowerPoint presentation that have somehow been stretched into a few hundred pages.

What Mark offers in the few hundred pages you hold in your hand is a masterful book that includes depth, breadth, and elegant simplicity, with a new insight on every page. Along with the guidance he presents in the book, Mark encourages parents to take advantage of community resources, assuring us that parents of any financial means can raise resilient, successful kids. Further, *How Children Thrive* is written to fit into parents' busy lives. You can read just a few pages at a time before falling asleep after a long day of work and play.

Beginning with a clear description of what executive function actually is, the book unfolds into an explanation of how we can cultivate executive function and resilience in our children, thus building healthy, happy brains and bodies to last a lifetime. With real-world advice about screens and other distractions, Mark understands the challenges the 21st century presents to all parents and families. And with his advice on self-care and mindfulness for busy parents, he truly helps us put on our own oxygen mask and breathe so that we can best attend to our families.

It is my wish for you that you treasure this book, and in so doing have children who grow up to treasure their own childhood and lives as they continue to thrive.

Christopher Willard, PsyD
Cambridge, Massachusetts

Introduction

LIFE AS A PARENT may sometimes feel full of pressure and chaos, but it is my hope that this book offers more simplicity and ease instead. By understanding how children develop self-management skills—various cognitive abilities that build resilience—so much falls into place about our family life. Parenting is complicated and full of uncertainty, but when we stick to what helps children thrive and let go of much of the rest, our lives and theirs become far easier.

Specific developmental skills act like the CEO of a business, keeping track of the big picture. They are involved with coordinating any life experience that requires persistence, planning, and organization. They are vital for problem-solving, navigating social situations, and monitoring our own behavior. They also dictate much of how children learn in the average classroom and how they manage daily routines. These skills, together often called executive function, or EF, as I refer to it in this book, tie together everything for parents, from the why and how of discipline to easier bedtimes to explaining the real-world benefits of mindfulness. A growing body of research shows that strong executive function sets up children for lifelong success.

Modern family life has become more complicated than ever, especially as we find ourselves increasingly bombarded with advice about raising children. Pushed to extremes, we are given the impression that even the smallest decision, from buying a toy to taking a swim class, may have a lasting effect on our children. The pressure to be the perfect parent is overwhelming. But the truth is, the job is too challenging and varied to ever be done to perfection.

Far too often, a deluge of contradictory information bogs us down rather than helps us make decisions clearer. Everyone from our mother-in-law to our best friend to the author of the hottest celebrity advice book claims to know best. We scramble to keep up with the latest recommendations, even though practically no one seems to agree on how to raise children. You're either pro this or anti that; parenting itself has become political. Overly strident online discussion makes us feel that if we do not listen to what *they* say, mayhem will fall upon our homes.

As a parent and developmental pediatrician, I have found that by moving above the swamp of advice, product placement, and Internet-driven anxiety, there is a more straightforward way to raise children. The world changes, but kids stay the same. At the heart of this book lies a developmental path related to self-management skills—executive function. Most kids walk near one year old, talk near one year old, and eventually learn to handle themselves responsibly—but not right away. When we stick to the common-sense, proven essentials shared in this book, life gets simpler and children become far more likely to thrive.

Attending to simple truths, tying together decades-old experience with cutting-edge research about children, we can let our minds rest knowing we have done our best. Plenty of practical science shows what impacts development most. There are few absolutes, but thankfully, between what has proven useful and what has been shown unhelpful, there's a lot of open ground to be ourselves. As it turns out, much of what supports children simplifies modern living—guiding children toward resilience and happiness doesn't mean one *more* thing to do—it's quite often one thing (or more) less.

Part 1 of *How Children Thrive* outlines the developmental path of executive function as it unfolds across childhood. As you'll soon see, understanding the development of executive function all on its own eases life for parents. Part 2 describes how to encourage the development of EF in children, and part 3 integrates EF into straightforward, evidence-based advice around daily challenges like sleep, nutrition, managing technology, discipline, and more. Finally, because practicing mindfulness directly builds EF, part 4 guides parents around mindfulness and family. Each chapter in the book is concise, can be read on its own (helpful if you get too busy for a while to read the whole book), and ends with something concrete to reflect on or try.

With the executive function–based insights provided in this book, you'll discover a more relaxed, balanced way to raise children. My hope is that you'll also have more fun, without getting lost in parenting worry, swept up in fads, or giving in to pressure to push your children too far or too soon. Child development is a path—and often a winding one. Yet there is an easier way forward. When we meet children exactly where they are developmentally, they flourish and find the balance and joy that allows them to thrive.

Part I

BRAIN MANAGEMENT AS A DEVELOPMENTAL PATH

*

Parenting can be exhausting and demanding, but it is a lot less stressful if you don't worry about every choice you make. People have been successfully raising children for thousands of years, using all sorts of styles, and many of them were less experienced, well-read, or intelligent than you. Understand the basics of how children develop and what builds their own independence, and let go whenever possible of all the rest.

Marshmallows and
the Developing Mind

FOR THE KIDS, let's start with marshmallows. Why marshmallows? Because it turns out that the basic cognitive skill of putting off a short-term reward (one marshmallow) for a long-term gain (two marshmallows) correlates with success across a lifetime. It reflects one step on a developmental self-management path called executive function (EF). Understanding the impact of EF in everyday life simplifies almost everything about raising children.

In 1972, Walter Mischel, PhD, then at Stanford University, published an influential and widely discussed study on delayed gratification in young children,[1] which relates to early EF. Preschoolers were brought one at a time into a nearly empty room with a researcher. The adult almost immediately received a phone call and said she must leave for a moment. On a table within reach of the child was a marshmallow. Before leaving, the adult set the child up for a challenge, saying, "You can have the treat now, but if you wait until I come back in a few minutes . . . then you can have two."

As you might expect, with the adult away, the children wrestled with themselves. They sat on their hands, covered their eyes, and scrambled to fight temptation. One group, the high delayers, managed their desires successfully—they struggled but ultimately earned a second treat. Another group, the low delayers, barely made it at all—*Marshmallow . . . got to have it now.*

Amazingly enough, Dr. Mischel and his colleagues were able to follow these children through high school and into adulthood. Unsurprisingly, perhaps, the low delayers had more behavioral problems in preschool than the high delayers. Interesting, but there's more. Followed into school age, this single preschool measure of self-management correlated with academic success.[2] The high delayers did better again. Into adulthood, it even correlated with an ability to maintain a healthy weight—the low delayers tended to have more difficulty with weight as adults.[3]

Of course, no one study defines much of anything on its own, but other researchers have added even more evidence that preschoolers with stronger self-management skills do better academically—all the way through their education. Attention is another aspect of executive function that has been studied. One publication showed that a child's ability to focus in preschool made it more likely she would graduate college on time.[4] The pattern is clear: Early self-management skills significantly predict future success.

Clearly, not every child who struggles with marshmallows will struggle in life. Some children may have their own, quite mature reasons, for being content with a single marshmallow. But these studies are quite significant—well, food for thought. They demonstrate that the bedrock of raising happy and resilient children rests on the developmental path of executive function.

EF refers to our mental capacity to manage just about everything in life, like the conductor of an orchestra, setting the path, keeping track of details, and running the show. A business requires *both* talented employees *and* someone to organize and coordinate the big picture. In the same way, all people require not only specific skills to handle routines, academics, social situations, and the rest of life, but also the ability to manage and hold it all together, to juggle tasks, and to overcome obstacles. EF involves skills like decision-making, self-monitoring, and planning. And this all begins to take root in childhood along a developmental path related to EF.

Executive function isn't yet a part of everyday language—*How's your son's EF maturing?* But it will be as parents better understand the role it plays in childhood. And here's the most reassuring point: Despite its wonky, overly scientific name, there is nothing complicated about building executive function. It's more straightforward and less anxiety provoking than much of what we're led to believe nowadays about raising kids.

When you start seeing parenting through the developmental lens of EF, you discover proven ways children learn, overcome adversity, get along with others, and become independent. It allows you to let go of so much of what is unnecessary, out of your control, and causes unwarranted fear. As a foundation, children require stable homes, clear limits, a time to play . . . and, for many, not much more than that! That's because, as you'll see, supporting EF, guiding children toward the ability to defer gratification, and more, not only makes their lives easier—it makes parents' lives simpler too.

Consider This

What you really want, and need, is an honest, objective understanding of child development for yourself, through which you will discover the choices that best fit your family. Kids have been raised countless ways by countless adults and overcome countless circumstances through countless generations. Step back periodically and see if you can separate the pressures created by the world around you from your own beliefs about what your child needs to thrive.

Managing Your Child's Brain—
Until They Can Manage It Themselves

EXECUTIVE FUNCTION resides primarily in the front part of the brain. It drives learning, monitors our thinking and behavior, identifies mistakes, and defines a host of other self-regulatory tasks essential to everyday life. In essence, its job is to integrate what we encounter in life with what we know and then decide how to respond. Like a good manager, it synchronizes our inner and outer experience and keeps us on track toward our goals. Before EF matures, a child understandably relies on their parents to provide guidance, problem-solve, and supervise behavior—acting as the brain manager while helping a child build their own independent skills.

Beyond what we know and have learned, and even beyond motivation, all of us require mental tools that let us plan and adapt to the challenges we face. Those cognitive abilities—the capacity to oversee our own behavior, anticipate the future, problem-solve, and coordinate just about anything that requires coordination—are all part of EF. Resilience and independence largely rely on this concrete skill set.

Executive function explains the link between so many topics on the minds of anyone working with children today. Terms like *mindfulness, resilience, grit, mindset*, and even *attention-deficit/hyperactivity disorder* all converge around the development of EF. EF-based parenting guides everything from common-sense behavioral management (young children learn almost exclusively from immediate feedback and not through discussion) to supporting teenagers as they mature into adults (EF, and therefore all of judgment and planning, mature only after teens become grown-ups).

Since the Stanford Marshmallow Experiment, discussed in the prior chapter, early childhood EF has been further linked to the well-being of adolescents and adults. One study even connected preschool executive function to adult measures of health, wealth, and the likelihood of getting into trouble with the law.[5] A strong brain manager guides performance not only in school but in recreational activities, personal relationships, and navigating emotions. Thus, supporting self-management goes a long way to setting our children up for success.

Until recently, many scientists believed that "development" ended in childhood. EF itself was a mysterious set of skills that popped up at some point and then stayed stable through life. Now we know that the skills required to manage life progress from infancy until almost age *thirty*. Normal human development continues far later than ever imagined.

Medical advances have turned other old-fashioned views of the brain on their collective ear. Whereas we used to think the brain barely changed over time, it turns out the brain responds to experience, like a muscle. On a neurological level, it adapts throughout our lives, a concept called neuroplasticity. Anything we do repetitively hardwires itself, from good habits to less useful ones. This includes either cultivating or undermining attention as well as cultivating or undermining EF.

Therefore, we now know: (1) EF is a developmental path that progresses through adulthood, and (2) the brain reorganizes itself throughout our lives (neuroplasticity). Let's tie those two ideas together, which will clarify both why EF is influenced by parenting and why it influences parenting.

Your child's brain develops for thirty years, and how you parent and the life your child lives affects brain development. This may sound stressful, but it needn't be. That's because *what affects EF trends away from pressured overscheduled children toward balanced, more successful ones*, allowing both you and your child to breathe easier. Your awareness of EF facilitates your decision-making around family scheduling, discipline, and much more. Becoming *aware* of EF, shifting perspective in this way alone and focusing on what works, is a powerful way to invite more calm into your family routine.

As an example, let's return now to the idea of EF and behavior, particularly discipline. A toddler cannot relate a delayed punishment to a current misbehavior; their brain is not yet wired to do that. This means there's no need for you to stress if they cannot reflect on the *why* of a behavior or do not change their choices much when you talk with them about why not to act out. In a toddler, a behavior happens, and whatever happens next (praise versus a time-out, for example) encourages more or less of it—that's all. This is EF awareness in action.

What about teens? EF explains why they need their parents almost as much as younger children. They crave independence, but with immature EF they often fail to consider long-sighted consequences of their actions—*Let's drag race, there's hardly ever any traffic on this road.* They don't have a brain manager fully on the job yet to moderate their emotions while also considering any larger implications.

Seeing the reality of teen EF doesn't mean we need to coddle or overprotect. Instead, we stay aware of our children's actual abilities while steadily offering more freedom and responsibility only as they show themselves ready. We let go of guilt and keep our children safe by respecting both their desire for independence and the relative immaturity of their growing brains.

Like any aspect of cognitive development, an undefinable amount of EF is genetically programmed and therefore outside our control—one of the fundamental stresses of parenthood. Yet much is influenced by upbringing and environment, and that's where our most effective efforts lie. For example, one of the most significant decisions in our busy tech-driven lives is protecting free play, the kind that flows from the imagination of children. Open-ended play itself evolved largely to support the growth of EF, and it doesn't require a lot of planning. In this way and others, EF-based parenting does not add anything *more* to most family schedules, it eases life in the long run.

What are the actual skills that go into EF? Language, walking, and running develop at their own pace, and so does the ability to manage life. It's useful to see how these abilities unfold. For starters, EF is often broken down into these three attributes:[6]

Cognitive flexibility (*The last fourteen times we had this discussion, we fought terribly. Maybe I should take a different approach.*)

Inhibition (*I'd like to bop you in the nose for taking my toy, but I'll talk to the teacher instead.*)

Working memory (*My mom said to go upstairs, get dressed, and come back down again. Oh, wait, what was that first thing again?*)

A more practical framework defines EF as related to six skill sets:[7]

Attention management: the ability to sustain focus when challenged, shift attention, and avoid hyper-focusing (becoming too absorbed) when engaged in an enjoyable task

Action management: the ability to control behavior, self-monitor, and learn from mistakes

Task management: the ability to organize, plan, prioritize, and manage time

Information management: the ability to remember, organize, and retrieve information

Emotional management: the ability to experience emotions without impulsively acting on them

Effort management: the ability to persevere when activities are challenging, sustain focus, and work efficiently

When stresses arise, across each of these skill sets you can ask: What does it mean for my bright, sweet-natured six-year-old child that she is twenty years away from mature EF?

At age six, your child is not fully able to focus, think of the future, or make a plan. Nor is she able to manage emotions or sustain effort when things get tough as much as she will one day. From that perspective, we can identify specific skills that require our support each step along the way.

To paraphrase an old saying, we cannot cover the road ahead for our children with leather, but we can equip them with a solid pair of hiking shoes. Instead of impossibly aiming to control and predict everything, we aim for our children to be capable of managing life themselves. Seeing EF pragmatically lays out the details of successful discipline, the capacity for independence, and what goes into managing the average classroom. At its heart, executive function encompasses our capacity to overcome the unavoidable stresses of daily life. As much as anything else we offer, taking time to support a child's emerging EF skills allows not only them but also entire families to thrive.

Consider This

The intention of this book is to offer another framework that will help you let go of whatever has been making life unnecessarily complicated when it comes to parenting. Many things we have learned in life support wise choices ... but not all. Much of what we believe may be because of how we were raised, what we hear from friends, or what we read on the Internet, where stories presented as fact are increasingly not based in reality at all. One useful practice is this: For any belief you have about yourself, your child, or the world, pause and ask yourself, *Is it true?* Consider what you are doing with your family out of habit that you might choose to change, while holding on to what is really valid and useful.

Putting One Foot in Front of the Other: Monitoring Milestones

YEARS AGO, a cartoon in *The New Yorker* showed two young children in a thoroughly trashed kitchen. There's a rake, a saw, and a garden hose, along with every pot, bowl, and condiment in the world scattered about the room. The caption reads: "And *that's* how you make a peanut butter sandwich."

As well as anything, this one cartoon captures executive function as a developmental path—it's not just what you know in life (bread + stuff inside = sandwich). Many preschoolers can describe the ingredients that go into a favorite sandwich. When pressed, some high schoolers could get a meal on the table. By their twenties, some young adults even end up running a kitchen or restaurant. To function at that level requires having not only the *facts* of what sits inside a restaurant, which even a young child could tell you, but the *capacity* to manage the situation well too.

Separate from the specific items needed to make a meal, something essential goes into *planning* the meal. And when you pause and reflect on what's involved, there's a developmental path that becomes clear. You cannot expect a six-, sixteen-, or twenty-six-year-old to have the same abilities for managing a situation like getting themselves, or a bunch of people, fed. The same goes for any other challenge in life—so it's up to us to define appropriate expectations across every stage.

It's not that every child develops in the same cookie-cutter way. Kids will be kids, and there will always be some welcome variety. But most kids begin to speak around the same age and walk around the same age. Across various childhood abilities, specific paths exist that children typically follow step-by-step. Pediatric guidance stems largely from this one foundational concept: Child development is predictable in many ways.

Children crawl before they walk, and walk before they run. They say one word around their first birthday and by preschool speak in short sentences. If a child falls behind, we aim to catch them up. If a child zooms ahead, we applaud their precocious abilities and celebrate their advanced achievements.

Just as with walking and speaking, EF follows a path. Toddlers *begin* to learn impulse control, and therefore require firm discipline and supervision, but can't be blamed for acting impulsively. Preschoolers gain the capacity to take another person's perspective, before which the answer to the question "Can't you see you hurt her feelings?" is neurologically speaking "No." By school age, skills expand around sustaining attention, memory, planning, and other crucial abilities that underlie classroom learning of reading, writing, and math.

But there's much more to EF, such as skills for managing complex situations or planning long-term. Teens act like teens, making rash choices or becoming emotionally volatile, in large part because the parts of their brain responsible for judgment, planning, and impulse control aren't mature yet. We can't expect them to fully take care of themselves. Because of EF, we must have different expectations of a six-year-old and a sixteen-year-old, but also of that same teen and a twenty-six-year-old. Seeing that, we stand firm as the mature adult in the family, even when teens push back.

Here are some age markers, and their corresponding rough milestones, around EF:[8]

Infancy (up to one year)

- The ability to understand that an unseen object, such as a toy hidden from sight, exists. (This awareness is known as object permanence.)

- Inhibiting behavior, such as the capacity to not touch something when an adult says no, begins.

- Mental flexibility, such as simple problem-solving (like reaching around an obstruction to get to a toy), begins.

Toddler (up to three years)

- The capacity to focus on interactive and individual play begins.

- The abilities to hold ideas in mind (such as keeping track during imaginative play) and maintain flexible thought (following someone else's changes in imaginative play) emerge.

- Impulse control improves (*Don't hit!*).

- Problem-solving increases.

Preschool (up to five years)

- The ability to focus grows at roughly three to five minutes per year of age in early childhood, for example, spending approximately ten to fifteen minutes with a crafts activity. It's not a perfect number, though. The best marker is the ability to focus for age-expected play (keeping up with peers) and appropriately complete simple activities (like art projects and later basic board games).

- Following routines that differ between situations and locations increases, for example, *At home I can leave on my shoes, but at Grandma's house we take them off,* or *It's raining, so I need to wear boots instead of sneakers without throwing a tantrum.*

- Delaying gratification and controlling impulses grows, such as not having to eat a treat *right now* and not lashing out when frustrated in play.

- The capacity to hold ideas and rules in mind increases (*Red goes here; blue goes there*).

- Shifting perspective, such as seeing things from someone else's point of view or following along with rule changes, occurs more readily.

School age (up to twelve years)

- Improvement continues in attention, allowing for more interactive play, sustained turn-taking play (like board games), participating in and completing activities (like sports or art), and academics.

- Problem-solving, task management, and maintaining independence around routines both at home and in the classroom continue to improve.

- *Gradual* improvement exists in the capacity to manage a project or studying, maturing into adulthood. In early elementary school, most kids have limited ability to plan details and manage time over days or weeks. Nor do they know how to study yet. By high school, most students have learned how to handle a complex long-term assignment and techniques for studying, although many benefit from supportive instruction.

- Emotional awareness matures, as does the capacity to discuss and manage more challenging situations.

- The development starts of a "time window," the capacity to link behavior *now* to *before* and *later*. In preschool, the time horizon maxes out around fifteen to twenty minutes. At school age, it begins at around an hour, and only by middle school does it expand to cover days (but still not years). As you may imagine, seeing that children lack perspective on time may greatly impact how adults approach planning and discipline.

Adolescence and young adult (up to thirty years)

- Almost everything listed above, including attention, impulse control, problem-solving, managing complex academic tasks, and juggling complex workloads, continues to improve, with skills reaching full maturity between ages twenty-five and thirty.

- Cognitive flexibility (figuring out new solutions, thinking out of the box) and efficiency (speed and effectiveness handling complex tasks) increase.

- Task and information management continue to improve, including the capacity to handle and organize mental information, workloads, and long-term planning.

The path to mature EF is long and gradual, without defined yearly markers found for other aspects of development. We cannot say a child *must* have an exact ability to focus for a specific amount of time by age five. But they should focus *enough* to join in with play and classroom activities. Impulse control matures through early adulthood, and along the way must be strong enough to enable a child to get along with parents and peers. Skills mature year to year, tracking along with increasing demands of a child's social, academic, and family experience. The bottom line for EF is monitoring real-life experience as expectations evolve at home, school, and elsewhere for children, rather than monitoring for exact milestones.

 Consider This

As children mature, we teach them what we can, but deciding what to introduce is guided by age. You speak differently to a two-year-old than you do a ten-year-old for a reason. You can't teach someone to ride a bike who hasn't yet learned to walk or run. Just because modern society has decided to push children faster doesn't mean they can keep up. Children have been developing all on their own since the beginning of time (or at least since the beginning of humanity), and sometimes letting them be exactly the age they are, in exactly the way they are naturally developing, best sets them up for success.

Kids Just Need to Be Kids

KIDS TODAY are the same as ever: They need to run around, fall down, play with friends, negotiate disagreements, and sort out what to do when their parents say no. They need to have fun and explore their world like all generations before.

For all the confusing, well-packaged dogma we encounter around child development, the basics remain unchanged: consistency at home, loving caregivers, steady boundaries, and limits. There's a reason several major companies have been successfully sued around claims that DVDs and other "cutting-edge" technology promote child development—they don't. Kids do not require more and more stuff that we buy them; they need to be kept safe and allowed lots of time to explore.

Nothing has changed through the years about kids themselves, except the world in which they live. A bunch of grown-ups—the mysterious influencers—apparently decided that kids need to read in preschool, must spend a large part of their lives on a smartphone, and that going outside on their own isn't safe. The problem is, there's not much reality to any of that. What benefits kids today hasn't changed all that much from when we were kids or even when our grandparents were kids.

Nowadays there's so much pressure to schedule all of a child's time or not miss out on one more educational class or product or the insidious suggestion that setting limits is bad. Technology pulls, with often detrimental consequences, across multiple aspects of development. Unstructured play is left for the rare moments when we have forgotten to schedule anything and cannot find a device to plug into. Yet what children have traditionally done to entertain *themselves*—unplugged play—often sets them up for success more than almost anything else.

Dropping the pressured messages of modern parenting takes effort. There's a cloud looming over all of us suggesting that kids need more supervision and more scheduling. Or maybe you don't believe that exactly but somehow don't really trust that there's an actual downside to excessive video game play. Or you may have heard kids should never have limits around food or that sleep training is unsafe or countless other rumors presented as facts about children.

Changing our beliefs almost fights human nature, a trait called the "confirmation bias." Humans selectively seek out whatever confirms what they already believe (a tendency that occurs frequently around politics). When we encounter something that conflicts with what we assume true, it causes anxiety and we resist even harder.[9] To remain open to change requires a lot of self-awareness and effort.

What does that mean for parents? We make choices based on whatever we think we know. Many of those facts are useful and correct, but some probably aren't so accurate. We start worrying because our child isn't doing nearly as many extracurricular activities as everyone else, and our worry is based on the belief that without a busy life they'll fall behind. It could be true (it probably isn't), and it could be an insidious idea we've internalized that more is always better (far more likely).

Here's another example: Kids have become increasingly sheltered and sedentary, staying indoors, frequently in front of the computer or television, because of a perceived risk of letting them free outdoors. Yet statistics suggest that the risk of abduction or violence hasn't gotten worse in most American neighborhoods.[10] If there's something about your neighborhood or a real situation that actually puts your child at risk, of course avoid it—heed facts first. Quite often, though, we know in our hearts and minds that outdoor time and freedom to explore would be healthy, and then irrational fears skew our decision-making anyway.

From a child development perspective, there's a reason that play evolved in the first place. A combination of time outdoors, sports, imaginary play, board games, art, music, and anything else that requires concentration, following rules, social engagement, and a shifting perspective promotes cognitive growth. As you sift through all the adult-led classes and video games launched from someone else's imagination, remind yourself that when it comes to EF, encouraging nothing more than good old-fashioned play is where it starts. Adults supervise and set safe boundaries; kids take the lead.

Periodically, take a figurative breath, or a literal one. To make strong choices around play, technology, food, sleep, and other healthy habits, a child requires a strong brain manager—and that's our role. Right up until children prove themselves capable on their own, it's affectionate, consistent parents who set the stage for a healthy, successful childhood.

Seek out ways to emphasize family time together, time outdoors, and everything that builds executive function. Catch yourself when you're able, and notice the assumptions that drive your parenting choices and your lifestyle. What do you value? What do you want your kids to value themselves?

You can't force your child to like any single activity or type of play. Yet as the world pushes and pulls, stay steadfast within the activities you choose to emphasize. Go outside with your kids, or send them out to play on their own. Remember to set screen limits; as the easy out for effortless entertainment, screens tend to trump anything else. Let children find other ways to entertain themselves when they're bored—downtime may have as much value for child development as anything else on the weekly calendar.

Through it all, have fun! Steer your children toward whatever you'd most wish for them. One father I met guides a Friday-afternoon stickball game in the street to encourage nearby kids to come outside and play. Offer opportunities to explore the arts, sports, time outdoors, and whatever else engages your child, without being caught up in a need to plan each moment, push academics, or create a musical or athletic prodigy by age eight.

Of course, childhood is not only about play. Letting kids be kids means the freedom to develop at their own pace and act silly and explore, all while parents sustain appropriate expectations around healthy routines and behavior. Consistent daily routines in and of themselves support EF in many ways, and require an adult perspective to start.

Kids don't learn to self-regulate out of the blue. Allowing them to find their way around play choices and scheduling, or around health concerns like nutrition, sleep, and screen time, frequently overestimates their brain development. Whether around behavior, schoolwork, or health, early routines become lifetime habits and build self-management skills that persist into adulthood. As their brain manager, you assist and guide them until they show themselves capable along the way.

In a similar fashion, limits and discipline affect the brain. Allow independence and offer choices instead of strict rules when appropriate—*Do you want to shower now or after dinner . . . but not at all isn't an option*. When it's time for a boundary to be set, even when kids push back loudly, that doesn't mean we've done anything wrong. Being told it's time to put the screen down and go outside isn't what they want, but you know better. Most young kids cannot find their own way to a healthy bedtime routine or homework plan or anything else that requires mature EF without direct advice—and limit setting—from an adult.

It's a blessing, in a way, to get angry or disappointed within the safety of a loving home and then recover. This recovery is part of how resilience is developed. Remember that your family still cares for you and the world doesn't end even when there's a disagreement. Through experiencing limits (*You can't talk to grown-ups like that*), children learn to manage frustration, handle emotions, and defer gratification. Of course, when children become upset over our choices, it may cause us to cave in against our better judgment. But as tense and confusing as limit setting can become, remind yourself whenever needed that teaching your child through emotional warmth and clear limits is what sets children up for success.

The skills of EF one day will allow your child to persist and problem-solve when challenged by whatever you haven't anticipated. If something you've heard or seen or were raised to believe leads you down a path of parenting anxiety, return to the basics: Stay warm but firm, confident as a parent but not an indulgent friend; prioritize play; and remain emotionally available yet clear-sighted in limit setting. These are proven steps to cultivating a child's happiness, independence, and resilience.

Consider This

What community conversations about children drive your parenting stress? Pause when you hear about the next crisis for "kids today." How unique and how factual is what you've heard? Consider the possibility that what *feels* worrisome is nothing more than an unexamined belief or has been blown out of proportion. Stay flexible, catch yourself, and check common perceptions about children by continuing to ask yourself: *Is it true?*

Executive Function Every Day

THE IDEA of executive function may seem abstract, but it's a very practical concept. The words sound as dry as chalk, like what a bunch of academics debate over stale doughnuts. Yet it represents how each of us figures out how to manage life. The brain evolved a perspective that supervises and keeps track of the big picture, and EF is it. Put yourself in a child's shoes and consider these real-life situations:

- A teacher assigns a several-page project. How do you pace your work so it's not done last minute, and also avoid throwing a fit each time a part takes longer than anticipated?

- You have chores and homework, and you want to go play. How do you figure out where to start, stay on task, and avoid distractions while all the other kids play outside?

- A child takes the toy you've been playing with for the last half hour. You need it to continue your game, and she refuses to give it back. How do you resist knocking her down and grabbing it?

The bottom line is that EF represents a variety of skills needed to overcome obstacles and make good choices. As you've now read, it includes the ability to focus attention when needed, and for as long as needed. It involves learning from mistakes, coordinating activities, and planning for the future. It includes managing emotions and behavior. Kids need time to figure out the nitty gritty while wading through all the increasingly complex situations life throws their way. That's why kids need parents acting as their brain manager, so they can take their time growing up.

When you look at things this way, it's understandable that without grown-ups, most kids wouldn't eat as well as they should. They probably do not realize that staying up late means being cranky and tired the next day. They may not consider the consequences of carving their initials into the dining room table. They're kids, after all, and getting in trouble for wrecking furniture is one way they learn. Without us, and without limits and discipline, it would take a long time to see the implications of much of anything.

Expecting kids to act more maturely than possible at any particular age can be quite counterproductive. The phrase "You can't walk before you run" may be a cliché, but you also can't read before you achieve several steps that precede fluent reading—which, in part, relate to EF. The same goes for writing, math, homework, and morning routines.

Tracking the developmental trajectory of EF helps us better comprehend our children's lives. You would not expect a four-year-old to organize getting out the door for school. A preschooler could probably list the steps: Get dressed, have breakfast, brush teeth. But a preschooler cannot coordinate time, remember the details, or stay on task, whereas most teenagers manage mornings on their own. Much of what changes relates to EF.

Let's reflect for a moment on consequences of rushing children's development. In preschool, children advance around both social and life management skills that *eventually* serve them in a classroom, though most aren't ready for actual academics. A generation ago reading and writing were six-year-old skills, with a big push in first grade, not kindergarten. Society's expectations shifted, but nothing much has changed about our kids. Development still happens at its own unhurried pace.

Overly high expectations that can't be met create false fears that a child is behind developmentally. Not every kindergartener can sit in a structured academic setting, then listen and learn; they're geared for play. Many perfectly brilliant five-year-old students aren't ready to read or write. One common consequence of pushing children academically too early and expecting young children to behave like older children is the misdiagnosis of ADHD, or attention-deficit/hyperactivity disorder. ADHD itself is a disorder of executive function. For all the children who actually have it, false expectations around development make it seem that others have fallen behind when they have not, potentially leading to misdiagnosis.[11]

These expectations ramp up stress for both parents and kids. If someone suggests that reading is *supposed* to happen by age five, that creates a false benchmark, and you may end up wondering why your child struggles. If you've been led to believe that middle schools *should* assign two hours of homework, you may compare your own child's behavior to those misleading expectations. Unreasonable demands challenge students. Well-meaning kids who want to please adults also become stressed as they reach to handle more than whatever made sense in the first place.

The same applies when setting overly high expectations for older students. If a high schooler strives toward competitive colleges or other lofty goals, guide them toward a viable resume but also around personal health and a balanced lifestyle. Support a broader perspective, because the expectation of the high school and extended community—even for something as basic as sleep—may be utterly off base. Teens need lots of rest, but they encounter both crazy early school start times and huge homework loads. Place value on downtime and family time and whatever else contributes to overall well-being, because with a teen's EF, she may find it hard to do that herself. Support her goals, but neither you nor your child are going to gain from an unrealistic expectation that she has the life skills of an experienced CEO while wading through the pressures of high school.

A developmental view even explains why technology has potential benefits but a distinct downside when under-monitored by adults.[12] Screen time looks like intense concentration from the outside but provides constantly shifting content that encourages little sustained attention. Too much screen time has been linked to disrupted attention, compromised EF, and other childhood concerns. Well-used and well-moderated tech time is fine, but the implied assumption that anyone lacking a mature brain manager (all children) would handle screen time on their own sets up a developmental risk for kids.

Until recently, kindergarten screening included a child's ability to write their name, recite the alphabet, rhyme, and count. That's still appropriate, though some schools have added reading and writing into even pre-kindergarten settings. So how do you determine what your child needs? Take care of the bare facts, accept you'd rather your kids not be pushed at all, and then stick to your own personal view of what's best.

Here are some guidelines for sustaining age-appropriate expectations while acting as the loving brain manager your child requires to thrive:

Focus on building EF. In younger children, encourage skills through traditional play, along with lots of exposure to spoken language and books. Language is another major predictor of school success. Thankfully, another direct way to build organizational skills at any age is through the routines parents create. In other words, when life gets busy, the short-term solution of *adults* adjusting family routines (everything runs easier) is the same as the long-term solution (more independent kids with better EF).

Monitor the big picture. Allow for discussion and options, but keep a bottom-line focus on what makes sense. Don't expect kids to make rational choices about scheduling and daily health routines until they show those skills themselves. Talk to your kids often about, and demonstrate to them, whatever your family values most in life.

Be selective in scheduling. Plan activities, but stick to only a few. Specialization in sports, in particular, is not recommended for most children until late middle school. Too much baseball by age eight means they may burn out, get hurt . . . or fail to realize that tennis is their thing.

Seek support when children fall behind. Consider specific developmental intervention, academic classes, or tutoring if your child seems behind; early catch-up is better than later. Some children benefit from academic interventions or services like behavioral therapy, speech-language therapy, or occupational therapy.

Trust your own judgment. Whatever external pressures exist around you, come back to your own sense of what feels natural. Put your child's temperament first. If you are in a demographic that pushes kids faster than you would like, stick to your own ideals whenever possible. Find a middle path when you can between the reality of your community and your own perspective. Most concretely, act as the brain manager whenever needed because your child's ability to thrive greatly depends on that.

Watching development unfold requires patience and more patience. We'd love our child to have more mature EF, because we know how important it is. The same goes for reading, writing, soccer, dance, or any other skill. We teach what we can when we see an opportunity. At the same time, we can't force development to progress any more quickly than it wants. Resiliency builds from early success, and success itself relies on appropriate childhood expectations along the way.

> ### Consider This

Don't worry that you must get everything right because that is, of course, entirely impossible. Kids are remarkably resilient and will do well across a wide range of life experiences. There's no perfect—just an opportunity to explore, make mistakes, and adapt along the way. Notice when you find yourself comparing your child to other children or someone else's arbitrary expectation. Pause and make choices founded in what you feel is accurate and true.

Not Ready for Prime Time Preschool

PRESCHOOL is in many ways the beginning of executive function development. Average preschoolers start with little ability to focus, not much impulse control, and almost no ability to organize, problem-solve, or take the perspective of a peer. By school age, they play socially, treat others with kindness, and engage productively in a classroom. Kids enter preschool as toddlers and come out as students. How does that change happen? Largely through the maturation of EF, which is why for the average preschooler, free play is the work they most need.

Preschool is the first time children learn skills such as deferring gratification, the capacity to put themselves in someone else's shoes, regulating their emotions, and sustaining their attention. They are brilliant and loving and yet know little when it comes to EF.

Immature EF explains an awful lot about early childhood behavior. For toddlers, everything is immediate. A behavior happens for a reason: *I want that toy.* Whatever happens next either encourages or discourages it from happening more: *I want, I can't have, I will have a tantrum* . . . and then she either gets what she wants or doesn't.

Ever find yourself having a circular discussion with your toddler or preschooler? You probably already know that talk doesn't change behavior much in the short run: *You're making a scene—cut it out! You know better. When we get home, I'm going to tell your mom what you said.* The only effective influence on behavior at this age is direct reinforcement of what we like (*Nice job cleaning up*) and discouragement of what we don't (*If you don't listen, you're going into time-out*).

Remaining positive and affectionate, as well as explaining yourself, are important ways of cultivating relationships and sharing your larger perspective long-term but do not much impact immediate behavior.

It's normal for children at this age not to recognize the implications of their actions. What they do now does not connect with later, and punishment later doesn't connect to behavior now. Therefore, it's not being cold for you to be direct with them, because their brains are wired to receive information directly in order to learn from mistakes. When it comes to discipline, immediacy is best.

Around social interactions, a famous preschool study that relates to behavior examines a concept called "theory of mind"—the ability to take someone else's point of view.[13] A young child sits in a room with an adult and is given a candy box. The child is shown that the box actually contains crayons. A friend—let's say Joanne—is going to come to join them at the table in a moment. The first child is then asked, "What will your friend Joanne think is in the candy box when she gets here?" Entering preschool, a child will say, "Crayons." Since the child cannot take Joanne's perspective, he thinks, *Of course Joanne knows it's not candy; I saw that clearly myself.* Closer to age four, a child's perspective expands and he sees things clearer—*Joanne will say it's candy because she didn't see the crayons and couldn't know what I know.* Before *that* growth happens, even the most empathetic preschooler would, if they could, probably answer the question, "Can't you see you hurt her feelings?" by honestly saying, "Of course not." They cannot yet be expected to take the other's point of view.

Discussion is well and good, over many years providing our adult perspective while building a communicative relationship, but it doesn't much impact short-term behavior. Due to typical brain development, the average preschool child doesn't have the sense to evaluate their own behavior across time or reflect on it as seen through someone else's eyes. For some, this holds true long into elementary school. Teaching appropriate behavior through discipline, encouraging what we like and discouraging what we don't, comes down to basic cause and effect. A behavior happens, and as adults we choose to encourage or discourage it from happening again.

As children graduate into kindergarten, EF underlies much of their ability to learn—the fundamental capacity to sit still and attend. Before that age, most kids aren't there yet. A precocious preschooler may love to read and write, but other equally healthy children may still be running around like lunatics and eating paste for fun and will almost certainly do just as well when they're ready.

More than figuring out good behavior alone, the developmental job of the average preschool student is *eventually* to pick up skills that let them learn in a classroom. As you've already read, one reason play evolved in the first place was almost certainly to augment EF. So the building blocks that lead to strong school-based skills are quite often actual wooden building blocks.

Educational guru Martha Bridge Denckla, MD, professor of neurology at Johns Hopkins University, has coined the concept "premature education" to describe the modern push for children to accomplish tasks before neurologically ready. While children are barely starting to figure out what it means to manage their own experience, we can't expect them to excel academically. Their brains aren't there yet. Premature academics don't work and, as mentioned, have been linked to the misdiagnosis of conditions like ADHD. Again, the pressure creates stress for kids and then adults who often falsely believe that the children are behind. When we emphasize typical development, starting with basic self-management skills, more children thrive when it's time, at their own pace.

A curriculum called Tools of the Mind has documented the benefits of preschool play.[14] The program focuses on self-management skills by emphasizing common games. Imaginative play has an important role, as it requires skills such as keeping ideas in mind, impulse control, and mental flexibility. Perhaps an adult sets up a scene in a restaurant, and then kids are prompted to switch roles (for example, playing the chef and then the customer) on the fly; this builds cognitive flexibility and the ability to change perspective, in this case around play but vital to problem-solving.

Through these old-fashioned play activities, children show significant improvement in executive function. Many traditional games encourage skills such as attention, impulse control, and flexibility and can be easily modified to require even more. An activity like Red Light, Green Light, for example, might start and then the rules switch (blue light, purple light), forcing children to pause, consider, and change their thinking. Despite debate about possible short-term academic gain, over time children graduating from developmentally oriented preschools (that emphasize play) seem to outperform kids from programs that focus on academics such as reading and math.[15] The link between play and EF likely shows why.

EF is vital to school success. If you're in a system that insists kindergarten is an academic year, of course try to build skills ahead of time that help your child succeed. There's no harm to introducing kids to letters and numbers, but leading up to kindergarten, exposure to books, play, and a focus on EF may go further in the long-run.

Keep it simple and fun. Read with your child, and provide lots of chances for open-ended, peer-driven play. If overall development progresses well, particularly around EF and language, have faith that your child will be more than ready for school when it's time.

> ## Consider This

Any time is a good time to take a breath and get back to what's truly important: enjoying your family. All this reading about child development can lead to overthinking. The goal of understanding EF is the opposite. Do your best, drop the extra stuff that's getting in the way, and then get down on the floor and enjoy time with your children.

School-Age EF:
Building Independence Through Routine

THE EMPEROR'S CHILD has no clothes. Look at him up there. He has a long school day and hours of homework. He plays a sport and the trombone. He supports a charity in his spare time. An exhausted crowd of parents follows along and tries to keep up with his torrid pace.

Ask many adults and they'll tell you that keeping up with their child's busy lifestyle feels like too much: too much homework, pressure to specialize in sports and music, and too much competition. And yet this is how our kids often live.

But which emperor is deciding on this schedule? Who made Little League baseball uber-competitive, five times a week, and with night games . . . for seven-year-olds? Who picked out the incomprehensible, overly test-driven school curriculum? Which emperor of parenting decreed that this is how anyone should live?

Pay attention for a moment and you will see that the emperor's child is naked and exposed. You can't change the world your family lives in, but you can change your own choices and perspective. See through the empty pressures, and find yourself a healthier balance instead.

Between kindergarten and high school, children's EF skills proceed through more than a decade of developmental growth from start to end. In first grade, children sit through very short stretches of lecture time and follow only basic classroom routines. Homework tends toward single worksheets. By eighth grade, class time grows longer, students manage projects and produce intricate papers, they collaborate with peers, and they also start to coordinate schoolwork with more and more after-school activities.

Nearly every aspect of learning requires robust executive function. Basic abilities such as organizing and processing information in a classroom rely on honed EF skills, like the ability for a child to take in what a teacher says, notice what's important, and integrate what they've heard with what they already know. The ability to focus, especially for unexciting activities, depends on executive function. Attending to reading details, holding information from the page in mind, organizing thoughts, and much of what's required for comprehension all stem from executive function.

Strong EF even protects children with specific learning disabilities, such as dyslexia. Children with reading difficulties and strong EF more easily compensate, such as keeping up with comprehension.[16] EF is used to master new situations and problem-solve and is called upon for any ability not yet learned to fluency. For a child behind in reading, their brain relies on EF to navigate the challenging task and fill in the gaps; for a fluent reader, minimal EF is needed. If a student lags in both the skill of reading and EF, they'll fall even further behind.

The capacity to gather thoughts a student hears and then mentally form a reply during a classroom conversation relies on executive function, as does the related task of coherently getting ideas down on paper. Writing is therefore another area of learning that relies on organizational and memory abilities rooted in EF. Without strong executive function, children struggle to produce clear sentences, paragraphs, and eventually essays and papers. Anyone challenged by early writing requires direct instruction in how to better plan the task, such as being shown how to outline or use a graphic organizer.

EF has little to do with intelligence, motivation, or academic potential but is the managerial ability that allows for success. As school progresses, children juggle an increasingly heavier load of projects and homework, afterschool activities, and other responsibilities. Through the start of high school for many, there's little ability to "self-advocate," a common buzzword in education, as that too requires EF-based forethought and planning. Our role as adults is to monitor individual skills in these areas and not expect too much too soon.

Executive function additionally relates to appropriate social behavior. As kids move through elementary school, peers expect them to follow rules, engage in play, and converse with ease. Tolerance wanes for anyone disruptive, as kids have far less ability than adults to be socially flexible. Later, maturing EF supports an ability to meet adult goals, such as achieving financial independence, following the law, and treating others with respect. EF in this way remains an integral part of development through adulthood.

Supporting an independent child and teen allows for whatever freedom and exploration seem safe and appropriate. When children start school, adults still act as the brain manager almost exclusively. In young teens, their skills stand on the threshold of greater independence, with some teens far ahead of others around judgment, planning, and EF. As teens grow, we mindfully give them more and more freedom, but only as they show themselves ready.

There's nothing wrong with allowing a child to explore and learn through experience when they seem able. Yet it's through simple routines, created by grown-ups, that much of EF grows at the start. Adults set the course, reinforce it, and fade involvement as a child truly becomes skilled on their own.

Here's a framework you can use to support children from preschool to high school:

1. **Adult creates and runs the routine for their child.** *Come over and let me show you the steps to getting this paper done.* Once a child seems to be picking up the skill . . .

2. **Adult completes the routine with their child.** *Come over and show me how you are going to get this paper done.* Once a child seems to be completing the routine mostly on their own (over days, months, or even years) . . .

3. **Child completes the routine with adult monitoring.** From a comfortable but close distance, you go about your day but keep an eye on progress. *Did you plan that paper? Let me see.*

4. **If the routine breaks down . . . return to the top.** *Oh wait, you haven't gotten started on that paper yet? Let's take a look together.*

You're the boss up until your child proves otherwise. You support EF by creating systems and routines that reinforce habits until they become hardwired, in essence passing on your brain-management ability to your child. School-age kids have *increasing* capacity to handle responsibilities, but largely rely on you. Whatever expectations the world seems to impose, keep your own expectations reasonable and developmentally realistic along the way.

> ## Consider This
>
> Part of the stress and reality of being a parent is that not every child develops in exactly the same way. Yours may need more or less support than your peers' children. Let your child, not outside pressures, guide you to the best decisions.

Keeping Homework in Its Place

THE COOL, CRISP FALL has arrived. The beauty of leaves changing colors carpets the land. And the anguished cries of parents and children wrestling with the nationwide trend for more and more homework fill the air.

Homework demands are up, although educational research doesn't much back the value of this trend.[17] Excessive homework creates stress, contributes to sleep deprivation, and takes away from family time and playtime. Homework is meant to support classroom learning and basic work habits—nothing more. It's an illusion that heavy workloads even in high school correlate with college success.[18] When home*work* takes over home*life*, it no longer benefits.

Kept in its place, homework gradually builds independent work habits and reinforces classroom material—that's all. Waiting for those skills to mature, your child's adult brain manager (you) is called upon for homework timing, organization, studying, and project management, especially when a school assigns a lot of it. Ideally, parents (and teachers) support strong habits, then fade their involvement as children become more motivated and independent. Eventually, children internalize and own the routines for themselves.

In moderation, homework can reinforce prioritizing, planning, time management, and other academic skills. Through middle school for many students, and into high school for others—particularly those behind in the development of EF—these skills grow from adult-provided plans. EF-based skills grow when adults set the groundwork and then allow more freedom as children show themselves capable.

If homework remains an ongoing drain in your child's life, seek advice. It might mean nothing more than a need for additional adult instruction. For anyone with immature EF (again, most young kids), their ability to create, sustain, and adapt plans isn't established yet, which means solutions must flow top-down from adults. If that's not your strength, consider involving a favorite teacher, tutor, or other professional. Discuss the situation with your child's teachers, as appropriately assigned homework should require minimal adult support. If the material is too hard, it's very possible that it's not the right homework at all.

In high school and even into college, students have less mature EF than adults. Force a college workload on a high school schedule, and demands may become entirely unrealistic. High school tends to be tightly scheduled, with a full day in the classroom. College includes far fewer class hours paired with lots of unstructured time for independent work. Expecting someone in a high school classroom eight hours a day to do three hours of homework makes far less sense than asking the same of an older student. High school goes better when, in addition to studying, students get enough exercise and sleep, and can chill out and spend time with family and friends. Balancing all that, along with their drive for a social life, ideally involves discussion and support from parents.

Of course, however you yourself feel about homework, you can't ignore the world around you. If your school district piles on homework, advocate whenever possible for a more reasoned approach. Find like-minded parents and see what you can change. And when the fearful idea pops up that your child will be at a disadvantage with less schoolwork, notice that irrational voice of anxiety, and remember it's simply not true. Create an environment that supports academic success, and assist wherever needed, but don't believe the useless hype about homework.

In spite of growing pressure otherwise, a parent's role in homework should typically be limited to making sure their child has a homework routine and watching that it is followed, answering specific questions that arise, and seeing to it that homework goes back in the backpack to be taken to school. Here is a list of some other helpful things you can do around homework:

Monitor homework time. The national recommendation for homework is around ten minutes maximum per grade,[19] meaning ten minutes starting in first grade and adding from there. Excess homework undermines long-term motivation for many and amplifies stress for almost all. Pushing younger children simply does not make them more likely to succeed later in handling tough workloads because they don't have the same EF-based skills they'll one day have to handle the chore. Children always manage best with age-appropriate expectations along the way.

If homework takes much longer than the guidelines, confirm your school's expectations and see if they add up. Nowadays many schools routinely exceed the ten-minute guideline, which you may not be able to change. But if your child consistently takes longer than her classmates, explore with school staff or someone outside the school (like a psychologist or pediatrician) what causes the difficulties.

Make certain the work is understandable. Homework is meant to reinforce classroom activities, not introduce new concepts. If a child does not understand, the content should be modified. If possible, avoid doing homework for your child or getting too involved; teachers better see what to teach when work reveals a child's true abilities.

Create a routine. A consistent routine established early saves years of arguing and dissent, calming homework stress over time. *We do homework when we get home from school like we brush our teeth before bedtime.* Completing schoolwork before play, screen time, or other activities teaches prioritization. Most kids understandably pick fun first and then frequently struggle transitioning back. Encourage playdates and after-school activities, but day by day steer back to the concept of responsibilities first.

Most effective for most children is to arrive home, take a breather, and then get schoolwork done. Modify this routine around after-school activities, but the same premise holds: Whenever your child gets home, let them take a short rest before they get down to schoolwork. As the night goes on, children (and parents) tire, efficiency and tolerance wane, and battles to transition back to schoolwork grow.

Teach organizational skills. Set up a clean work area, with minimal distraction. Use day planners and calendars to demonstrate to-do lists, time management, and other related skills. A wall calendar that tracks the family schedule provides a great visual support for children starting to understand time. Many children need direct advice—or limits set—to permit appropriate computer use without distraction from schoolwork.

Consider a checklist for completing homework:

__ Check what's due.

__ Check that you have what you need.

__ Complete your homework.

__ Check your work.

__ Put your homework away.

Parents start out heavily involved, and over time transition to more general supervision. "Have you completed your checklist yet?" becomes enough to make sure everything gets done.

If organization remains a challenge for you as a parent, do your best. As long as your child does well, there's nothing to worry about. If difficulty arises, seek support from a professional for yourself or your children. Collaborate with school staff to make certain materials and assignments get back and forth, and discuss other available supports. Not everyone is skilled at everything, and it is no judgment on a parent to seek help.

> Consider This

When homework persistently consumes your child's life, pause and reflect. Appropriate homework can be completed independently (apart from occasional questions to clarify) in an appropriate amount of time. When that isn't happening, ask teachers to adjust assignments—and consider whether your child might need work on a specific skill, developmentally, academically, or around attention and executive function.

Adolescent Brains Aren't Grown-Up Brains: Collaborating with Your Teen

ADOLESCENTS ARE CALLED "adolescents" for a reason—they are not yet grown up.

For all the joy of watching our children grow toward adulthood, along the way most teens don't manage life or make choices maturely practically by definition. Everything from juggling busy schedules to making smart choices online will be impacted by the fact that most don't have mature executive function skills quite yet. They yearn for full independence. It's normal to strive for separation from parents and to experiment with defining themselves in funky, unique ways. It's also normal to have shortsighted judgment or for reactive emotion (sometimes referred to as our primordial "lizard brain") to win out over our more complex "human" brain before it matures.

Puberty brings a burst of cognitive development (seen particularly in long-term thinking, planning, and impulse control) that ends sometime when young adults reach their mid to late twenties. You may know a teen ahead of the curve who seems ready to run a corporation, but most adolescents won't be grown up for another ten years or so. Our job is to guide them. They'll never admit it, but they depend on us for that. We encourage exploration and growth, and our involvement continues until teens prove themselves responsible.

Teens become uniquely vulnerable. They are defining their personalities and considering their futures. Emotions rocket up and down, and social lives feel fickle. While they push away from us on one level, they depend on us on a far deeper one. Executive function, the basis of forethought and planning, does not typically become fully established until adulthood. From this point of view, it makes total sense that a brilliant but emotional sixteen-year-old with the EF of an average sixteen-year-old makes an impulsive, regrettable decision to text a naked photo of herself to a crush. Or she might cave in to peer pressure and get into a car with an impaired driver.

Throw teen emotions, hormones, and social intensity into a mix with immature EF and you define the need for involved adults. Teens may not see the long-term implications of getting a facial tattoo or texting something nasty about a peer. They might not fully grasp the intense content available online or in games or in the news. And they certainly miss the basic importance of details like getting enough sleep and eating well. They can have the intellectual capacity to tackle academics without an equal ability to handle emotions or the logistics of their high school scene.

What are the implications for parents when teens push for independence but remain immature around forethought and planning? Stay positive and connected whenever possible, and stick to fun family time when you can. Encourage exploration, independence, and choice, but gauge the limits of your teen's judgment. Not every high school student is ready to plan and run their own life. Adapt and meet them where they are developmentally by collaborating where possible and letting them make mistakes, all while sustaining a firm grasp of your role in monitoring, setting limits, and perhaps (when allowed) providing wisdom.

Parenting a teen often feels terrifying because we can't control their lives. Thankfully, generations have stepped into the emotional and developmental intensity of adolescence and come out on the other side. The following guidelines offer a collaborative approach to supporting independence in teens:

> **Allow for independence … to a point.** Incrementally offer an increasing amount of freedom while monitoring the bigger picture. Let teens find their way and learn from their mistakes, which are essential for learning, all while knowing you're around to make sure whatever happens isn't insurmountable. Provide freedom while remaining a resourceful parent to fall back on when needed.

You can't expect mature decision-making from an immature brain. For any emergent skill in life, inconsistency is to be expected. Every moment of clarity (a stunningly executed science project, for example) may be followed by another of confusion (such as a pressured choice to stay out late before a test). It doesn't mean we should not let teens have smartphones or drive a car. It does mean that we proactively want to give guidance about how to use them appropriately, set limits, and monitor their progress along the way.

Collaborate in decision-making. Collaboration often requires a clear range of what makes sense and is permissible—options and choices—but not allowing a teenager to completely fall on her face. Encourage discussion when difficulties arise, and let teens take the first crack at problem-solving. Even through that process, recognize when they require a defined boundary. If they prove ahead of their peers, try and adapt to that. If they prove to need support and limits, step in and set those. Self-advocacy itself—seeking guidance from adults or peers when troubles arise—requires EF, so parents and teachers reaching out and following through can make a lot more sense than watching and waiting.

Set limits. Teens often require boundaries around behavior, health, technology, and other areas of their lives. Hopefully, they never bump up against these restrictions, but for safety's sake they exist. In fact, teen behavior sometimes tests the safety net just to make sure we're there to catch them. They push a boundary, we set a limit, they get upset, and yet there's reassurance we were looking out for them too.

Monitor the big picture. Encourage a lifestyle that allows for family time, downtime, exercise, and sleep. Routines like regular family meals and rules around technology have been shown to benefit teens behaviorally and academically. Remain flexible, but also use your adult EF (remember, you are still the brain manager) to provide advice, model healthy habits, and set household standards. You cannot, and should not, aim to control everything, but do selectively influence what you can.

As much as teens strive to be grown up, they still are teens. Brilliant, well versed, and yet without mature EF, they misbehave, they collapse under stress, and they fail to come up with a useful plan when the wheels (perhaps literally) fall off. EF is the backbone of everything and waits for them once they really, truly become adults.

 Consider This

Understanding EF doesn't mean oppressing our teens. Encourage discussion and let them explore, all while keeping a firm sense of their actual self-management skills. Stay a parent, offer responsibility and independence gradually, and keep a firm grasp of your own role as the family brain manager.

You Gotta Take Care of Yourself

TAKING TIME FOR YOURSELF supports not only your own well-being but drastically changes the lives of your children. Frazzled, over-stressed parents make for frazzled and overstressed families. You may feel the need to be on call all the time, but there is no advantage to 24/7 parenting—it's another unique stress for the modern parent. No one can be available all day, every day, without becoming awfully tired and run-down.[20]

Having one child is demanding, having more than one child even more so. Even if your kids are, against the odds, each and every one an angel, the logistics of getting them out of bed, dressed, fed, out the door, and then back inside at a reasonable time—while continuing to do all the grown-up chores you've always had—may, in the end, create even more parenting pressure.

Parenting can feel like one big sloppy mess, especially since family life never goes exactly as we pictured. A huge school project that you were told is due next month is due tomorrow, *and* you forgot to buy the chicken part of the chicken dish you're cooking, *and* you haven't exercised in a month, *and* you wonder if your son forgot to bring his soccer bag to practice yet again. There's always one more thing to fuss about, it seems, or to do or fix or change.

There's also nothing most of us care more about than our children. Just having them causes most parents a fair amount of worry about their well-being. Add on chronic sleep deprivation and shattered routines around eating, exercise, and sex. Altogether, becoming a parent creates a thriving medium for a great deal of stress.

Our interconnected, media-driven world often amplifies that parenting stress. Knowledge and reassurance about raising children in the past came from an intimate group: family, close friends, and a pediatrician. Extended family provided a network of support, yet these days it is rare if multiple generations all live in the same town. Instead, we reach out to our peers, many of whom are just as inexperienced as we are . . . and to the Internet, the great perpetrator of fear.

Turning on a faucet of information to sate ourselves today is more like unleashing a fire hose. A quick drink to slake our thirst for knowledge blasts us with a deluge of confusion. Rose-colored postings online about why each child is more precious and advanced than every other one leads us to doubt our more realistically inconsistent lives. We are led to believe there is so much we "must" do or our children will fall behind or suffer.

We desperately want happy and successful children but can't control everything. In real life, inevitable surprises and unexpected moments arrive on our doorstep. Perhaps we have one picture of the future, but our kids disagree. Right when we think we are doing okay for a moment, another online posting about a child reading novels at six while playing classical violin makes us wonder why our child draws crayon stick figures.

A kind of implied judgment looms. Beyond falsely perfect postings, there may be pressure to meet standards that don't fit for you. You may want to breastfeed, find yourself unable, and then have to deal with all sorts of negative feedback about using formula. (While breastfeeding is recommended, most kids do well with either.) Or you may need to return to work sooner than your parents think you should, or you find that your friends choose to work but you want to stay home instead.

Fear insidiously ends up driving our lives. Every catastrophe anywhere in the world has become part of our local experience. The overall rate of anything bad happening to kids hasn't shifted much, if any, in the past fifty years, though it feels much worse. A twenty-four-hour-a-day media industry streams horrific headlines and hooks us with quick fixes to problems both real and imagined.

And lastly, far too often we get swept up by viral trends carried by some perception that they will save our kids (from what, it isn't clear)—all based on fads and salesmanship and television ratings and social media. An endless stream of often-conflicting information has created a parenting culture of unease that won't abate. Yet if you feel pressured to handle anything exactly by the book (this one or any other), you're going to exhaust yourself even more.

All that anxiety around raising children isn't without consequence. When we're overwhelmed, it affects how we act and think. Stress triggers our fight-or-flight response. *I'm in danger and must protect myself.* Evolutionarily speaking, that might pertain to, say, being chased down by a terrifying predator. Nowadays, it tends to mean something more abstract. *I wonder if anyone will notice the stain on my son's shirt at the concert tonight.* There's a brain-based on-off switch when it comes to stress, and all too often it remains endlessly stuck in the on position.

Chronic stress undermines our mental health and our physical health, and it changes how we think. One study even suggested that one of the best measures of a child's stress is their parents' stress level.[21] A reasonable amount of stress keeps us on our toes and motivated, but when it comes to stress and family, it's all downhill from there.

There's a further implication to undermanaged stress: The often-unspoken last part of fight or flight is a mental "freeze." Under danger, who needs to deliberate? *No time to figure it out—gotta run.* We stop thinking clearly. We fall back on reactive habits, which might be a perfectly reasonable survival tactic (*Run away, there's a lion*) or not so much (*Run away, homework has to get done*).

Adult EF defines how well we handle challenges ourselves, and stress and burnout undermine our parental EF. Stress causes less flexible problem-solving and a decreased capacity to sustain effort (like sticking to intentions around discipline or a new homework routine). That state of depletion makes managing family life harder, creating a cycle that sustains our exhaustion. If we don't find time to build our own resilience, we create patterns that perpetuate themselves.

Whenever family life seems unstable and overly (as opposed to routinely) chaotic, a valuable first step to hitting the reset button may be a few minutes to take care of yourself. Rediscovering your own strength, or simply taking a moment to settle, is often exactly the next best step to taking care of your child.

Here are a few self-care strategies to consider:

Value what keeps you healthy. Find one activity that keeps you sane and strong, and no matter how busy you are, make it happen. Music, reading, hiking, movies, knitting, or whatever you choose, stick to it. Pay attention to how you budget your time, how you eat, and how you take care of your body—and whenever you can, make lifestyle changes that reduce overscheduling. Strengthen yourself so that you have more energy for your family. It's not for you alone; when children are part of family life, they pick up similar healthy habits.

Notice what's right. As with children, adult resilience relies on acknowledging what you do well, instead of wallowing in self-judgment. Take small, steady steps toward change, pushing back against mental habits like perfectionism and negativity. Play to your strengths and allow for long-term, steady progress toward family goals.

Value relationships. It's easy for spouses to lose track of the little free time they spend together. Months, or even years, after having children, they may find their relationship strained or distant. If you have the resources (and not everyone does), schedule a regular babysitting night so that you and your significant other can go out and do something grown up. Or trade nights of babysitting with another family. In the same way, and particularly if you're a single parent, find times for friends as consistently as you're able. Creating this time also embodies healthy relationships for your children, letting them see the importance of treating others with warmth and compassion.

▶ Consider This

There's an adage around rock climbing: If you find a solid hold that allows for a rest, take a break. Who knows the next time rest will be available? Throughout your day, and your life, when you see a chance, take a breather. Instead of continually doing and fixing and, of course, checking social media and email and succumbing to the pull of the average smartphone, actively choose something that allows you a restorative minute or two.

Part 2

THE **A-E-I-O-U** AND **Y** OF CHILDHOOD WELL-BEING

＊

What matters most in raising happy and resilient kids? Coming back to the basics, parents can focus on their A-E-I-O-Us: **A**ctivities, **E**nvironment, **I**nstruction, **O**ld-fashioned education, **U**nderstanding when to intervene (for children who fall behind), and **Y** we work hard. Use these concepts to build resilience, promote executive function, and keep your child on the path to success.

A IS FOR ACTIVITIES

Prioritizing What Matters Most

THE DAY ENDS and you pull into your driveway. You open the mailbox and, groaning, take out a two-inch pile of mail, 90 percent junk, but needing to be sorted. Riffling through it as you walk, there are, of course, several bills, one of which says, "Second Notice." How did that happen?

Your spouse is upstairs working while the babysitter plays downstairs with your son. There is a note on the table: "It's your turn to make dinner." Apparently, you were supposed to do the shopping. Time to order in again.

As you throw your keys onto the table, you see the note you wrote yourself to call the painter who hasn't come to finish his work in several months. The dentist, you remember out of the blue, you forgot that callback too. And one more business call awaits, left over from your day. Oh, and the dishwasher should be emptied, and the garbage . . . and a mental fog slowly settles on the evening.

Except your child awaits, and you promised to play ball with him when you got home. But there's a pull; everything would sure feel better if the to-do list got done—for once. Or maybe not. Taking a breath, you leave the rest for later. Your son gets his promised time together. You'll sort out dinner, and the to-do list can wait until after his bedtime.

*

Healthy living starts with stepping out of autopilot. Our lives may feel driven by the need to plan, control, and not miss out on an activity that might cause our children to fall behind. Yet in a calmer moment, we might recognize little of that to be true. Often we are living quite differently than what we'd recommend to anyone asking our advice.

The solution starts with pausing, checking in, and prioritizing. For ourselves, that means finding what keeps us sane in the midst of family demands. For children, that means emphasizing whatever they most need and enjoy and setting aside much of the rest.

Outside of fun time, social time, and school, what do children actually require? When it comes to executive function, various everyday activities relate to its growth. Anything emphasizing sustained concentration builds attention; the fractured, rapidly skipping attention created by media does not. For a family, that means, in a gentle way, starting with reading, imaginative play, art, sports, board games, and similar activities. As you'll soon see, in early childhood, both unplugged, engaged play and reading are particularly vital steps toward school success.

Of course, we should not (and cannot) force children to enjoy an activity because it's good for them any more than we can force someone to like brussels sprouts. Instead, by patiently exploring various options, sticking to priorities, and creating boundaries about what's healthy, children discover their own interests in time. One message may be, for example, that everyone exercises, so it doesn't matter what you sign up for, but you stay active somehow.

Beyond enjoyable activities, how we spend our time in other ways matters too. Research shows family meals alone correlate with fewer behavioral problems.[1] Healthy sleep, exercise, and quality nutrition may contribute to long-term development. And, of course, when with your children, you can emphasize on a moment-by-moment level giving them your full attention whenever you're able.

Periodically pause and reassess your family time. What could you cut or simplify? Using a daily calendar and blank paper, use the following exercise to help you prioritize your family's schedule.

1. **Lay out your family's schedule as it is now.** On a daily calendar or blank paper, record a typical weekday and a weekend day. Get into the details. For each family member, include when everyone wakes and goes to bed

and unavoidable logistics, like cooking, cleaning, your job, homework, and getting ready for school. Estimate time spent checking email, surfing the web, playing games, and watching television, as well as time spent on recreation, driving, and all the rest of the family's logistics.

2. **Create a new calendar from scratch.** On a second blank page, record what you'd like to prioritize first. Start with what's nonnegotiable—school hours, bedtime, homework, or anything else that may not change right now, noting what's actually fixed (the bus comes at 6:50 a.m.) versus what's adjustable (bedtime at 8:30 p.m. might work better this year).

3. **Fill in next what you value most.** Include whatever you choose to prioritize, for yourself and your children, like exercise, spending time with friends or family, reading, creative pursuits, after-school activities and social time, and engaging in fun and positive activities together. Make sure to include your self-care, and schedule downtime for your children if that tends to get lost in the shuffle.

4. **Consider what to do with any unscheduled time.** Time remaining is potentially available for nonessential activities: another after-school activity, television or video games, or whatever has been consuming family time. Or leave that time blank, and see what happens.

Whatever you prioritize, your children will more likely do so too over time. If you want your child to be a reader, they must see you reading a *book*, not a screen, since on a device they have no idea if you're playing a first-person shooter or reading a novel. If you want them to seek out open-ended playtime, hiking, museums, exercise, or anything else, childhood habits begin with how parents schedule their families through the years.

Consider This

You already know what is best, even if the pressures of life temporarily get in the way of carrying through. Break the inertia by pausing and starting over with your schedule. Dedicate time to what's required, protect time for what you value, and create a plan that meets the temperament of you and your family.

The Vital Role of Play

"If it weren't for time-outs, I'd have no free time at all."
THE NEW YORKER CARTOON

LIKE MOST CHILDHOOD SKILLS, EF grows largely from our genetics and is then influenced by our upbringing. Therefore, our children's EF can potentially be enhanced or hindered depending on our choices as parents. For everything that may impact EF—from mindfulness to computer games to physical exercise—our decisions around play may have the largest immediate effect.

The fear that we need to micromanage life to avoid missing out on anything at all distracts from what sets children up for success. There's nothing wrong with classes for learning and fun, but too many pull kids from being kids. A music or art class, where children follow closely what they're asked to do, has its own value. Executive function grows more from self-driven play, supervised by adults but with kids left to create, imagine, and negotiate on their own.

We protect playtime in our busy tech-driven lives not only for fun (though it is) but because free play itself guides executive function.[2] Imaginative games, for example, require working memory to keep track of the details (*We're going to the moon*), cognitive flexibility to follow along with changes (*Now we're pirates*), and impulse control (*Wait, I wanted to stay out in space*). Video games, exciting and engaging as they are, provide mostly passive entertainment—someone else has imagined the worlds we explore.

Studies in the emerging field of EF have found potential benefits from a range of activities, including exercise; games requiring strategy and concentration (such as chess); curricula that directly teach aspects of executive function; and the practice of mindfulness, through which focus and awareness are built intentionally, much like physical exercise. However, the beginning, middle, and end of supporting executive function in childhood is valuing, scheduling, and promoting good old-fashioned play.

For adults, following a child's lead in play doesn't always feel easy or straightforward. One behavioral program called Parent-Child Interaction Therapy suggests following the PRIDE acronym when you feel less than engaged.[3] Get involved, show kids you care, and (as always) don't overthink life. Sit down, run around, and have fun with your child.

> **P = Praise.** Encourage appropriate behaviors by giving immediate feedback. "What a cool idea that is!"
>
> **R = Reflect.** Repeat back and provide commentary on what your child says and does. "So, Josephine is a good witch now? How did she change?"
>
> **I = Imitate.** Copy your child when she plays. If she imagines her dolls taking the bus to school, participate and follow along. If she draws pictures, draw your own.
>
> **D = Describe.** Show interest and expand your child's vocabulary by describing what you see. "Isabella is on an adventure? Who is she going to see?"
>
> **E = Enjoy.** Display enthusiasm about whatever your child is saying and doing while you play together. Catch yourself when you get distracted and bored, notice where your thoughts have gone, and if it's time for play together, jump back in.

When kids seem to want mostly more and more screen time, what's a parent to do? Have the types of games you want at home, steer kids toward them when you can, and play them with your child. Once again, set rules about tech time, as it draws kids away from other types of play. Technology is perfectly fine in moderation when you supervise the content, but if traditional play is integral to your home life, kids learn to connect with those games too.

The following activities and game suggestions divided by age and adapted from Harvard University provide ways for kids to enhance and practice their EF skills.[4]

Toddler

- Simple games such as peekaboo and rhyming/finger play games (like pat-a-cake)

- Hiding games (like hide-and-seek or hiding toys) and copying games (imitating an adult)

- Role-playing

- Conversation of any kind with an adult

Preschool

- Active games such as follow-the-leader and freeze dance

- Song games and finger/hand play games

- Conversation, storytelling, and role-playing

- Matching and sorting games

- Arts and crafts

- Imaginary play

School age

- Card games and board games

- Active games such as Red Light, Green Light, Mother May I? Simon Says

- Ball games such as four square, Gaga, dodgeball, and, for older kids, organized sports

- Movement and song games

- Puzzles, brainteasers, logic games, guessing games, strategy games

- Music, singing, art and dance

- Reading

High school

- All of the above, of course: reading, music, sports, art, logic games, etc.

- Crossword puzzles and math games (Sudoku)

- Exercise and getting enough sleep

> ## Consider This

Many kids seem to have lost the habit of entertaining themselves—it takes no mental effort to turn on a screen. Almost anything else does, including reading, board games, making up a game outside, or practically any nontech activity. Build an "I'm bored" play box: Create notecards for all the age-appropriate activities you imagine possible, pulling from the list above. When your child complains of boredom, send them to pick from the box. Sometimes a card makes them think of something else to do instead: *An art project? I'm going outside.* That's perfect!

Putting Your Kids on a Media Diet

WITH ALL THE FOCUS on independence and self-management, what disrupts executive function most? A 2011 study compared nine minutes of watching a rapidly moving undersea cartoon to either an educational television show or doing a crafts activity.[5] After the cartoon only, there was measurable worsening of EF . . . and who shuts off a show before ten minutes? Similar studies show a direct correlation between increased time in front of screens and poor EF.

The entire point of EF-based parenting is a healthier, happier life. We want our children to think for themselves, focus and behave, to develop healthy sleep and nutrition habits, and to do well in school. Excess screen time has been shown to undermine each of those goals. The good news is, with strong parental involvement—setting rules about when, how much, and what content is appropriate—the ill effects of technology vanish.

The drive toward more and more technology is not like the advent of rock and roll, an inevitable generational change embraced by youth in the 1950s and 1960s that many adults feared would be a harmful influence (not to mention a threat to American class values). It's more like this: In the 1950s smoking was everywhere. Doctors even appeared in ads for cigarettes. Big Tobacco pushed smoking into everyday life through active campaigns that hooked children. Far too late, realization grew that smoking was associated with numerous health risks and thus cause for public concern.

Repeatedly, in the last century, a developing industry defined its place—and only afterward did our society realize the need for boundaries. If a substance in our water supply were to become linked to obesity, poor academics, aggressive behavior, and early sexuality, there would be a public uproar. Yet that "substance" is here. Television and video games have been linked to all these problems, and more. A generation from now, what are we going to think about having let it happen? Our children are lab rats experiencing its impact on their development, for better or worse.

Study after study tells us that exposure to inappropriate screen time is associated with negative outcomes. By one estimate, having any electronic device in the bedroom, including television or a cell phone, robs an hour of much-needed sleep a night. Too much device time displaces other healthy pursuits too, whether physical (children have become increasing sedentary), social (more time on social media has been linked to decreased happiness), or academic (more screen time pulls from reading time).

There seems to be a community-wide assumption that around technology, there's nothing to be done. Television and computers are everywhere—airports, pediatric offices, automobiles, multiple rooms of most homes, and in everyone's pocket. Meanwhile, evidence grows monthly that it puts our children at risk. The newest and latest can be fun. It can increase productivity, support fitness habits, and all the rest—but we're better off when making choices about how technology integrates into life rather than letting it happen to us.

Here's the bare fact: The expansion of technology is not a harmless trend. The industry thrives by using psychology to its advantage, fine-tuning products that make us crave more. It's not like asbestos, something to banish entirely, but instead requires careful contemplation. For modern kids, a healthy relationship with media has become as vital to promote as discussing sleep, exercise, and nutrition.

Technology can help parents and kids remain socially engaged, or it can disrupt social engagement. It can support organization or contribute to daily stress and chaos. It can benignly provide entertainment or disruptively draw from healthy play. And, of course, it can either educate or utterly undermine learning. Without involved adults, kids don't have the EF-based judgment to figure it out.

Technology is both a tool and a product that can be implemented wisely or mindlessly. We need to *manage* its use—something challenging even for adults with mature EF. For a child immature in planning and prioritizing and not yet monitoring short- and long-term consequences, impressionable and resoundingly influenced by marketing, screen time requires clear-sighted intention far beyond their capabilities. Firm parental guidance keeps screens in place and guides children toward a better future.

There was an eye-opening blog years ago containing an unexpected message from Apple founder Steve Jobs.[6] Jobs stunned a reporter who asked, "So, your kids must love the iPad?" with this answer: "They haven't used it. We limit how much technology our kids use at home." The genius who brought us the iPad protected his own kids from its influence.

Jobs's intuitive remark echoes a message that professionals have inconsistently gotten across for years: Parents must protect kids from too much screen time. One estimate puts the amount of time spent between ages eight and eighteen at 7.5 hours *a day*. Surveys show that 72 percent of children go to bed at night in a room with at least one electronic device at their disposal.[7]

A study out of the University of California suggests that this trend in technology inhibits the ability to recognize emotion.[8] Sixth graders who went cold turkey from technology during five days at a camp became significantly better at reading facial expressions than a group who carried on life as usual, attached to smartphones, iPads, computers, and television. Children who better understand their emotional and social experience develop more positive relationships. As a species, we evolved through face-to-face interaction. All evidence suggests kids learn better from live interaction than screens.

Stress caused specifically by smartphones impacts parents too.[9] Suddenly we are meant to be available to children, work, friends, and even social media feeds 24/7. There is a deluge of information and a constant strain to split our attention. No one can be on call all the time without burning out, and for parents it creates an expanding sense of stress and exhaustion.

This is not a call to reject all technology. Used appropriately, it can be a wonderful part of our lives. Instead of passivity, we can make certain that children (and parents too) use it more sensibly. Parental monitoring of media *does* work and has specific, positive results around children's sleeping habits, school performance, social interaction, and behavior, as well as on the development of EF and the brain.

What would happen if we all paused, considered, and made active choices about technology? Instead of riding the wave, we can specifically decide what would be healthiest and feel best.

Consider right now the *who, what, when, where*, and *why* of your child's tech time:

Who: Act as role a model. Instead of remaining on autopilot and letting technology happen, approach it with awareness and openness to change. It's a product meant to grab attention, whether or not that's in our best interest. Pause, check in with yourself, and resolve to use technology skillfully during family time.

What: Decide on appropriate content. Content and marketing significantly influence children, but the industry-created rating system doesn't have much value. Use neutral observers such as Common Sense Media (commonsensemedia.org). Unless Common Sense (or another neutral site) says something is age-appropriate, it's off-limits. Parents cannot play or watch everything, so let someone else take the reins.

When: Decide how much is appropriate. Children have a hard time managing screens because, well, they're children. There aren't many games or websites that politely ask a child to stop after an appropriate time. It's up to you. Emphasize your values and set a firm limit on daily screen time. The more consistent you act, the less discussion and fighting you'll experience through the years.

Where: Set up a central station for a media bedtime. Create a place where all laptops, tablets, and phones end up at the end of the day. Recharging devices outside the range of the bedroom will better recharge people for the next day. It also goes without saying that all media should be kept out of the bedroom. Enhance your children's sleep habits by powering down exposure to all screens an hour before bedtime.

Why: Value healthy pursuits over media time. An hour less time spent on games and social media may mean an hour more spent outdoors, reading, or doing art. Set aside time for whatever play you value before determining screen time boundaries. Some families find that no screen time during the school week makes everything run easier. Beyond all that, consider tech-free days or vacations on a regular basis.

Consider screen time a privilege, not a right. Decades ago, frustrating though it was, inappropriate behavior while driving might have led a parent to take the car keys. If kids misbehaved, they could get grounded—forced to stay home and disconnect socially a night or two. If you take away favorite devices for a short time as a teaching point, kids will only learn from the experience. From preschool to high school, children must follow your rules aimed at staying healthy and safe.

> ## Consider This

Seventy percent of children feel their parents should be in front of screens less. Monitor your own use. (As an experiment, use an app to monitor this for several days.) Minimize devices during family time, meals, and downtime. Kids learn so much from watching their parents that the first step for our kids is to check our own screen habits.

E IS FOR ENVIRONMENT

Positive Parenting with Authority

POSITIVE PARENTING sounds like its own new age cliché, but it is actually quite an effective approach when coupled with clear limit setting. It largely means kids are better off when they get more encouraging feedback than negative. Sounds easy enough, but life gets busy, kids are challenging, and despite our best intentions, before we know it, our entire focus becomes corrective. Five things go right in the morning as our kids brush their teeth and get ready. Then they try to run out the door barefoot and the first thing they hear from us that day is, "What are you doing? Get your shoes on; we're late!"

Resilience itself relies on affectionate, consistent adults who guide children toward their strengths, teach skills, and provide a consistent emotional base. In our busy lives with our attention pulled countless ways, it's easy to take positive moments for granted and focus only on control and correction. A positive focus even when things are hard doesn't mean being fake—it acknowledges the fact that when life gets challenging, staying positive takes effort.

Kids benefit from clear limits and discipline too, so "positive parenting" means nothing more than balancing our feedback. Kids want to feel safe. And part of bonding is that you, as a parent, are protecting your child from the world. Part of doing that often means teaching children to accept disappointment. While in the moment they may get upset, in the bigger picture, they feel protected, secure, and loved.

Every parent needs various ways to guide their children. But all through high school, many kids learn most directly from experience, not so much from discussion. A behavior happens, and what happens next either encourages or discourages it from happening again. This immediate feedback starts with our approval when something goes well, reinforcing behaviors by acknowledging them with a gesture or kind word. With awareness and effort, we shift the focus of our feedback toward strengths and successes, which ultimately builds self-esteem.

Developmental psychologist Diana Baumrind created an enduring parenting framework in the 1960s. Under this framework, a "permissive parent" tends to be nonpunitive, often acting like a resource or a friend and not a consistent guide in shaping behavior. Rules are generally open for discussion, and children experience little household responsibility. Children are expected to regulate their own behavior, without necessarily adhering to any external standards . . . even though, as you've now seen, children with immature executive function cannot be expected to manage well without adult structure and support.

While an emphasis on warmth and connection has clear value, research suggests that overly permissive parenting puts children at risk for becoming impulsive, immature, and out of control. Inconsistent limit setting and indulgence may lead children to poor emotional regulation, low persistence when presented with challenges, and even defiant behaviors. Attachment, the basic connection between a child and caregiver, does not rely on avoiding all negative feedback and disappointment, although that fear often drives parents into a permissive style.

Authoritar*ian* parents attempt to control behavior based on preconceived rules, with obedience always expected and punitive measures primarily used as enforcement. Autonomy is limited, order and traditional structure maintained. There tends to be little discussion of rules or why they exist. While structure and consistency have benefits, children of authoritarian parents turn out to be at risk for becoming anxious or unhappy, and often have poor frustration tolerance.

Authorit*ative* parents strike a balance, directing behavior but encouraging discussion when possible, sharing their reasoning, and valuing *both* self-will and adhering to appropriate values. Children explore and question, but standards regarding behavior are maintained. Reasoning and group decisions are encouraged, with a firm understanding that parents often must make unilateral decisions. Children raised in this style are more likely to be resilient and self-confident, with strong emotional regulation, social skills, and sense of well-being.

How can we best sustain this balanced approach to positive parenting? For starters, it simply means prioritizing positive time together.

No matter how busy life gets, set aside enjoyable time and protect the activities you bond over. If you have more than one child, aim to find consistent time with each of them when you can.

Whenever possible, notice appropriate behaviors, recognize hard work, and reinforce what goes well. On autopilot, we often note only mistakes, maybe taking for granted fifteen minutes of quiet play but snapping when we're interrupted afterward. When it comes to feedback for kids, try to base your comments in reality; kids will see through anything falsely positive. For example, not every child needs a trophy for showing up.

Save rewards and positive feedback for *valid* effort and *real steps* your children take toward success. For example, crediting a paper full of mistakes only with, "Nice job, here's a gold star" may not be specific enough. "Nice hard work—you have a few words to correct, and then you'll get a star" links effort to positive outcomes. Even the spelling correction has a positive message, showing kids that it's fine to make mistakes if we're doing our best. Everything from healthy relationships to self-esteem relies on tying effort to successful outcomes.

If this overall emphasis on the positive feels lost within your family, pause for a moment. Where can you shift your own habitual responses? Is there a behavioral expectation at home that doesn't fit your child's skills? Sometimes it's nothing more than the chaos of life taking hold, and what's needed is a little more structure around how you manage behavior. Try writing down a specific plan that supports your aims. Don't blame yourself when you lose touch with these intentions—it happens to everyone. Instead, patiently come back, over and over again.

Positive parenting comprises three important tools listed below that complement limit setting and guide children toward success. These tools don't require being fake or always being your child's closest friend. Rather, they demonstrate that you are the parent; you're loving, emotionally available, and clear with demands.

> **Schedule consistent time together.** Of all behavioral guidance, this tool is the most general but the platform on which all the rest stands. Create time together that

your child depends on and during which he chooses the activity, either daily or weekly. Set aside a few consistent minutes, and never take them away as a punishment (*No matter how bad things feel, we still have this time together*). It's not a cliché that children often act out for attention. Giving your child the attention they long for and deserve may even defuse some challenging behaviors.

Use targeted praise. Make a practice of noticing even small things that have gone well (*Nice job listening*). Being positive means meeting our children right where they are in their development, and building success from there—not praising nothing, but focusing on effort and successful steps. False praise is empty praise. Targeted praise is more specific than general affection too, going out of our way to notice and label the *opposite* of problem behaviors.

Use reward systems. Remember, for some children, behavior is about immediacy all the way through high school—something happens and then gets reinforced or discouraged. Collaborate toward success by aiming for the opposite of problem behavior again; instead of "Don't hit," reward your child for using their hands appropriately. Even for a well-behaved child, encourage new routines by creating a checklist and rewarding its completion. Keep plans simple and prioritize one step at a time instead of addressing everything at once; a stepwise plan allows children to feel more successful as they progress. Reinforce healthy habits, sustaining motivation for a child who otherwise might not see the value of what we are asking until after they experience it for themselves.

All parents require accessible tools to guide behavior, and even the most well-behaved kids benefit. When an easygoing child doesn't want to change a routine or pick up a new chore or habit, positive parenting techniques can come first instead of coercion. And whenever tension rises at home, returning to a more structured behavioral approach goes a long way toward finding calm again.

> ## Consider This

> You want your children to feel they are the center of *your* universe—not *the* universe. Start with validation, support, and a focus on the positive. When a child's actions trod on someone else's rights or happiness, getting in trouble is a teaching point. Staying positive never means losing touch with the larger messages you want your children to hear.

Limit-Setting Guides
Children Toward Success

IT'S NO LEAP of brilliance to remark that kids need consistent limits, yet we all struggle in different ways to implement them. Kids resist, often quite resourcefully. We want them to be happy, and we want to be happy ourselves, so we relent, perhaps because at that moment we're too run-down to rally. Maybe our neighbors set different standards and we worry that they'll judge us—or that our kids will. We may feel pushed to anticipate our kid's each and every need ahead of time, or perhaps we're inclined to treat teens how we would another adult. Not only do these ideals burn out parents, they fly in the face of what we know about cognitive development.

We absolutely want to minimize children's distress, maximize their well-being, and treat them with care and respect. The overriding goal is a warm, supportive environment that balances clear rules with open discussion when appropriate. The bottom line is that kids require clear limits for emotional growth, to develop resilience and frustration tolerance, and to learn how to interact with the world. As the grown-up in the room, we must always aim for what's best in the long haul.

Limits are in fact a large part of why kids need parents. If from the start children knew how to behave in public, eat a balanced diet, pick clothes for the weather, treat friends, manage time, handle responsibilities, and make healthy lifestyle choices, we could get them an apartment when they near kindergarten and leave them to it.

For now, our kids rely on us to mediate between them and the world, protect them, and teach them as they grow. Part of our role is to cultivate EF-related skills such as emotional resilience, cognitive flexibility, and patience. Whenever they leave our home, life will present challenges and we won't be there to referee.

Our standards sometimes lead to an upset child. That reaction does not mean we've let our child down or are being "mean." Children may feel—and won't hesitate to let us know—that we wreck their lives by denying them the newest video game or cool shoes. It's not fair that the kid next door stays up later. Maintaining open-minded objectivity, taking stock, we stand by our judgment of what is appropriate.

Short-run battles lead to long-term prevention. Would we deprive a child who steps on a nail a tetanus shot because he screams a blue streak? Of course not. The reality is, children can get incredibly upset over almost anything. And one common flash point is when they encounter a limit, such as "It's bedtime now" or "You can go out to play when your homework is done" or "You can't push your sister—go take a time-out." We're rarely doing a child a favor by overindulging them or caving into their whims.

Moving down a path to independence depends on parents teaching boundaries and allowing kids to encounter occasional frustration. Common-sense, old-fashioned sayings such as "Life isn't always fair" and "You can't have one just because your friend has one" may appear out of vogue but are what science suggests children need to hear at times to thrive. These experiences shape brain development.

Clear limit setting is therefore inherent to positive EF-based parenting. When we truly pay attention to our children—recognizing temperament and abilities, knowing likes and dislikes, and responding to their maturing development—we discover an evolving necessity for rules and guidance. At two years, at ten, and at adolescence, the details change, yet upholding limits remains one of the most essential, loving parenting skills required of us.

That all may seem obvious, but what gets in the way of our limit setting? Our own exhaustion, for one. Parents who immerse themselves in rearing children without any acknowledgment of their own needs are at risk for burnout.

Stress itself often leads to inconsistent limits and a general state of overindulged children: "Yes, you can have the whole box of cookies for all I care as long as you let me finish this phone call." Setting aside a few minutes a day to meditate or hang out with a friend or schedule a date night with our spouse can go a long way toward establishing consistency with our kids. An important aspect of setting limits for kids is understanding our own.

Overestimating EF is another common problem that undermines discipline. A child's apparent misbehavior may stem from not yet knowing how to manage emotions or the morning routine. Another quick path to *actual* misbehavior is asking for something a child is not capable of doing. He may unconsciously think, *That's a big pile of homework . . . I don't know where to start.* It makes utter sense for him to throw a fit if he's pushed to work but doesn't know what to do—he needs us to step in and support him while creating a reasonable plan. He might need guidance in breaking the homework into smaller portions and managing time. Perhaps we need to talk to his teachers about adjusting his assignments. Maybe a potential learning difference requires more of our attention.

Maintaining rules and guidelines does not mean becoming rigidly strict. Guide behavior through reward and praise whenever possible. Have fun, make jokes. Offer reasonable options: "You can do your homework now or in half an hour but not right before you go to bed." Pay attention to your choices and stick to only as many limits as needed. Remain open to discussion and flexible to change, but adhere to clear boundaries the remainder of the time.

Coordinate with caregivers and teachers around your plan to manage behavior whenever possible. When will you rely on time-outs? When will you use ignoring as a strategy? When is it time for consequences? The more structured you are in managing behavior as a parent, the easier it is to stay calm and consistent under pressure.

Record your strategy somewhere easily accessible, and consider posting it for your children. Remain aware that with any change around discipline, your child's behavior may intensify for several days or weeks. Once the new plan takes hold, the whole household will run more smoothly.

Remember, establishing healthy attachments and relationships stems from emotional reliability from you, not protecting your child from ever getting upset. It's okay if kids get in trouble or don't succeed in everything. Your child isn't perfect and needn't strive for that goal. Positive parenting requires an emphasis on supportive feedback while continuing to teach children through firm boundaries and limit setting.

You are the adult. You get to say no and set rules when you must. This is part of being a mindful, caring parent. So what are the limit-setting tools to rely on?

Time-Outs. All parents need a behavioral tool that can be repeated multiple times a day on occasion. Typically, major consequences shift behavior only once a day. After declaring, "You're grounded this weekend," what can you add? Yelling doesn't work, and physical punishment is out. Time-outs are irreplaceable—a few minutes sitting somewhere boring to settle down. With persistence and planning, they work for almost all families (for more details, see 134).

Redirect Behaviors When Possible. Because every behavior happens for a reason, it's easier to replace a behavior (*When you're angry, go to your room*) than squash it (*Never throw a tantrum like that again, ever*). For your child, simply stopping a reaction is far harder than shifting the impulse. When there's room, offer choices, targeted praise, and rewards to define new behaviors that replace problematic ones. A sense of control for a child goes a long way. Asking a child to clean up *right now* may lead to conflict. Ask if they'd like to clean *now* or in *five minutes*. They'll choose later, feel better, and become far more likely to clean up.

Planned Ignoring. Childhood behavior often derives from a desire to grab attention or change a parent's mind. Even negative attention from an adult may feel better than no attention. For instance, if a child is jealous of a sibling, acting out may allow them to own your attention for a minute or two. When a behavior is attention seeking, punishment or too much discussion can perpetuate it. Therefore, if you don't respond at all to some behaviors, they resolve.

Not responding outwardly takes effort. To avoid seeming callous, calmly state your intention ("I'm going to wait until you're settled") and then move on. Your bile rises and a cloud impairs your vision, and you continue as if nothing is happening. The results are often worth it (although you should expect a short-term increase in the behavior before it resolves). This approach is especially effective with tantrums. In the face of unremitting screaming, parents understandably give in to demands: "Fine. Take my phone. Just quiet down!" That outcome makes the inappropriate behavior useful because the child receives what they want, even though they are being chastised. Rendering the behavior useless by ignoring it makes it less likely to recur.

Natural Consequences. Children sometimes learn from making a mistake and experiencing the outcome. Your child refuses to wear a jacket, so you let him go outside and get cold for a few minutes. He won't stop goofing around and as a result misses the beginning of his show. Instead of redirecting your child, you let him persist and experience whatever happens as the natural consequence. Of course, don't use this approach in situations where safety is at risk, only when the stakes are low.

To use natural consequences well, remain aware of your child's development. Natural consequences work only when a child has the underlying ability to manage a situation. "Fine, stay up late, you'll be sorry when you are tired tomorrow" doesn't affect much; most kids won't be able to relate how they'll feel tomorrow to today's actions. Even if they *say* they understand, they almost certainly *feel* otherwise, until they have a broader perspective of time and more advanced EF.

Whenever natural consequences fail, reevaluate your assumptions. You might think poor grades would be a solid natural consequence. But if a student is *unable* to handle her homework, they aren't. More often than it seems, even the brightest child relies on parents to set the groundwork, problem-solve, and create a solution.

Direct Consequences and Lost Privileges. During a calm, quiet moment, plan consequences that make sense as a fallback. Ones created on the fly often are unenforceable (*If you don't stop, we're flying home from vacation today*). Consequences can be loss of screen time, a favorite toy, an activity, or anything else feasible and clear in meaning. Whenever you find yourself relying excessively on consequences, step back and review your behavioral plan and be sure you're mixing it up. Households cannot stand for long on consequences alone.

*

Through all the corrections and conflicts children encounter, it's crucial to return to positive time together, positive feedback, and rewarding behaviors. Aim for consistency, forgive yourself for your own inconsistency, and start with a focus on the positive whenever possible. And then, with children of any age, remember that positive parenting techniques only go so far on their own—all parents need means for firm, dispassionate, and consistent ways to say no.

> ## Consider This

Within the safety of a supportive home, experiencing frustration is an opportunity to realize that stuff happens … but that life is going to work out. You wouldn't want a child who never overcame adversity in childhood. Or one who expects never to be frustrated or who never earned anything through actual effort. Limits teach self-management skills, as long as they're within an overall picture of warmth and connection.

Chronic Stress and Communication

STRESS IS AN INEVITABLE part of life. Problems happen—cars break down, computers crash, people come and go from our lives. Good things happen—new jobs, weddings, babies. All these events, in different ways, cause stress. And stress, of course, affects our families.

The nature of our communication itself captures the impact of stress on our family life. Recall a seriously tense, unpleasant conversation, something that made you feel utterly off. Visualize when your mental fight-or-flight or freeze response took over. Communicating effectively and calmly almost certainly became a serious challenge.

The effects of stress on the mind and body are well studied. Chronic stress leads to health issues as varied as elevated blood pressure, exacerbations of medical conditions, and mental health problems. In childhood, so-called toxic stress levels (such as abuse or living in a war zone) may even change how genes are expressed, affecting physiological reactions for a lifetime.[10] Reducing stress has direct benefits that make it more likely we will live longer and increase our chances of feeling happy and mentally sharp.

As parents or otherwise, there is no way to eliminate stress. Things change or do not work out like we expect, sometimes quite often. When researchers list stressful life events, even positive experiences mix at the top. In many ways, our minds have an unreasonable, preprogrammed expectation that the world will one day be fully under our control—and then stay that way. Since kids bring with them a lot of change and uncertainty, stress tags along too.

Much of what triggers our physical stress response is rooted in our amygdala, the fight-or-flight part of our brain. Fear is part of our survival instinct. Reflexively, we react and protect ourselves (*Uh-oh, I'm about to be run over by an elephant*). Because that reaction lets us leap away from danger, we cannot, and should not, annihilate this safety mechanism. We can, however, improve how we *manage* all the less life-threatening fears and anxieties inherent not only to parenting, but to life.

The amygdala itself has no innate intelligence. When it's activated, we're focused on self-protection and reflexive habits that require no mental effort. We don't want to methodically debate, turn things over, and waffle while in actual, acute danger. Since we're not thinking, we have tendencies we instead fall into when stressed. Someone eats, someone shuts down, and someone else lashes out at their family. We manage bedtime the same way for our second child as for our first, even though it is clearly ineffective this time. We are too harsh (or too lenient) about tantrums because of how our parents handled them.

To break these reactive cycles requires awareness of how they start: A thought is a thought, and not always worth stressing over. To remain an open-minded and flexible parent requires shutting off stress mode over and over again. We catch ourselves, settle, and become more intentional in how we manage our family life. We notice our habits and make more conscious choices. Where we always felt there was only one way to manage a situation, more options become apparent.

Returning now to stress and communicating with children: In any conversation, all we influence directly is our own behavior. Even when a child seems intentionally oppositional, managing what we say and do next affects everything that follows. This doesn't mean specifically staying quiet; perhaps there's a need to be more assertive under pressure. Without condoning a child's words or actions, we deescalate or escalate whatever comes next through how we listen and express ourselves.

Here, then, are some initial steps to take toward meaningful and less stressful communication:

> **Listen first.** Whenever possible, allow your child the opportunity to express his perspective. Then, if you disagree, pause and explain why.

> **Find a place of connection.** Start with agreement, particularly when you disagree and are going to set

a limit or try to convince a child to change a choice. (*I can see you want to stay out with your friends—that makes sense to me. You're upset about being grounded. I would be too.*) Or even simply, *I'm sorry you're frustrated.* In any situation, connect first if you're able.

Monitor your body language, posture, tone of voice, and facial expression. We often unconsciously undermine conversation through how we hold ourselves. When possible, align your body language with what you want to convey.

Monitor your emotional state and its influence. If you're feeling strong emotions or see that your child is, consider taking a break or having the discussion at another time.

Notice your expectations. If you find yourself making assumptions about your child's thoughts or what will be said next, aim to set them aside while listening.

Pause before and during speaking. Make sure your child is done speaking before you respond, and make sure you're heard when it's your turn. Ask for repetition or rephrasing if you are uncertain.

Allow for communication repair. Much of skillful communication relies on reflection afterward. There will always be times when you lose your cool or fail to get across what you intended. The same goes for your child. Allow time to settle, and when both of your stress levels are reasonable, try again.

Understanding the impact of undermanaged stress is another strong reminder around parenting and self-care. Don't let the thought that you're carrying too much stress create more stress. Stress is normal, and even has some value in keeping us motivated and safe. But you do want to take care of yourself enough and manage stress as skillfully as possible when you're able.

> ## Consider This

A 2015 study found that washing the dishes can be a stress-reducing break.[11] Instead of resenting the dishes or ruminating while cleaning, focus attention on the activity itself. Your mind will soon get caught up in whatever causes you anxiety or angst. Each time it does, refocus your attention on the task at hand. When washing dishes, notice the feel of the water, the soap, and other sensations, sights, and smells. Give yourself a several-minute break instead of using this mundane task to throw fuel on stressful fires. Settle yourself over and over throughout the day and see how that begins to affect your family experience.

I IS FOR INSTRUCTION

Training Your Brain
to Live More Intentionally

MANY OF THE CONCEPTS in this book—staying aware of your child's development, modeling compassion for children, working to reduce stress—relate to the idea of mindfulness. The word *mindful* has been used for hundreds of years, at its simplest to mean "aware." Being mindful reflects living a life where we pay attention to what drives our experience and how we relate to our world.

Mindfulness can be defined as being more fully aware of our experience in each moment, with less reactivity. A basic premise of it is that we spend a fair amount of time anywhere but here. With practice, we notice when we're lost in distraction and then come back—we aim to pay attention to what's actually going on right now more often. Without this type of awareness, what happens? We leap out of bed to get the kids to school and spend those few chaotic minutes with them thinking about our workday. At work, we fantasize about the weekend. Free for the weekend, we spend it worried about all that's unresolved at our job. Distracted in that way, we're on autopilot, doing and speaking and making choices around our children without giving any of it much useful attention at all.

One way to move away from this state of mind is through mindfulness meditation. This meditation style starts with attention. Our mind wanders and always will, and we train it to come back more often. It's not an attempt to escape from reality or to have a perfectly still mind. The long-term intention is well-being and wisdom, but the basic intention is even simpler: Getting out of autopilot, which mindlessly keeps us living life out of habit, benefits our families in countless ways by allowing us to live life more intentionally.

As a physician trained in Western medicine, I started integrating mindfulness into my practice as research increasingly defined its benefits. Studies show that people who practice mindfulness exhibit physical changes in their brain related to focus, emotional control, and compassion. Parents and children who practice mindfulness report feeling less stressed. Other research reveals physical and psychological benefits across dozens of health conditions. If that seems like snake oil, it shouldn't. Chronic, undermanaged stress exacerbates any health condition, and better stress management is one consistent result most people discover when practicing mindfulness.

And yet we practice mindfulness not just for better focus or less stress or more responsiveness. It's more like working out. We don't want stronger lungs or legs or arms alone—we want our body as a whole to stay in shape. With mindfulness, we support our entire well-being by settling ourselves and building our awareness, which improves life not only for us but for our family and anyone else we deal with day to day.

Most days, our mind goes off all over the place in spite of our best intentions. As you'll soon read, that habit makes us feel more worry, anger, and fear. But we can work with where our attention goes, not because we're forcing ourselves to feel "it's all good," but because seeing life clearly, with less reactivity, benefits us no matter what we may find.

Excited by the idea of training the brain, adults sometimes leap directly to, *How can I teach my children?* Yet children learn so much from how the adults around them live that you cannot skip over your own part. You *instruct* children in tying shoes and figuring out math. Mindfulness begins when you *embody* traits like responsiveness, attentiveness, and compassion through your own practice—one that starts with nothing more or less than taking the time to get out of autopilot and start living your life a whole new way.

Consider This

Commit to a daily practice (such as a focus on the breath, or walking mediation) for a stretch of time and observe what changes. Schedule a specific time daily, setting a reminder alarm. Notice when life gets in the way of these few minutes for yourself—and recommit each time. Make a note to check your progress several months from now. Set aside any perception that you can be good or bad at it (neither is possible), and just do it, as the saying goes.

Guided practices can be a great tool to get you started. Mine are available at howchildrenthrive.com.

PRACTICE   Breathing Meditation

If you're new to a mindfulness practice, one way to start is by focusing your mind on the physical sensation of breathing. You don't need to breathe any special way, fast or slow or otherwise, to practice mindfulness. There's nothing magical about it and there's nothing to force; the breath happens to be there all the time and is therefore a tool you can always use when distracted (which for most of us is quite often). As best as you're able, not expecting a totally still mind, notice the natural movements related to the breath moving in and out of your body. Recognize (and expect it) when your attention has wandered, and come back to breathing again.

Bringing Mindfulness Home

PARENTING IS A LONG, unpredictable road. There will be sunshine and storms, uphills and downs, grassy fields and muddy swamps to cross. There aren't any shortcuts. Day by day, everything changes. From the weather to all the pleasant, unpleasant, exciting, entertaining, and horrifying events that crop up, much remains utterly outside our influence. That road goes on, practically speaking, forever.

One option is to grasp for endless control. Aim to predict everything, anticipate everything, and protect our children from everything. When it rains, fill every puddle. When it's sunny, aim to blow away clouds gathering on the horizon. Or blindfold our children while they walk, shielding them from the reality that life can be tough, until one day they slip from our grasp and stumble out into the real world.

Of course, wrestling with life in all these ways won't work. Uncertainty and parenting go hand in hand. Resisting that fact inspires even more anxiety, fear, and anger. Battling what cannot change amplifies our unhappiness and exhaustion, blurring vision and obscuring from sight what is most useful for our children.

Enter mindfulness. We can't guarantee the road, but we can provide children tools to manage on their own. Whatever your image of mindfulness, it's nothing more or less than a direct way to handle the uncertainty of life. Don't worry if you cannot sit still—you don't have to sit still. Don't worry if your mind is often or always busy—that's true for everyone. Practice mindfulness because you're human, parenting is hard, and the traits you build with mindfulness will make it easier.

It's useful to think of mindfulness as a broad approach to life, a mindset, rather than one more thing you have to do in a day. It's less a singular activity than a whole package, a set of cognitive skills that develop with repetition and effort. Living mindfully includes all the ways you emphasize whatever makes it more likely your kids end up happy and resilient.

Stress itself occurs when life does not fit our picture of what *should* be. Which might mean something as huge as *I imagined I'd be in a happy marriage forever but now I'm getting divorced* or as simple as *I had my heart set on a cheeseburger but they are out of cheese.* Recently back from vacation, we may feel particularly magnanimous, accept our disappointment, and move forward. After an awful night's sleep and a fight with our boss, the no-cheese experience causes a meltdown. Whatever we face in life, our perspective matters.

According to Jon Kabat-Zinn, PhD, one of the fathers of mindfulness in the West, mindfulness is "the awareness that emerges through paying attention on purpose, in the present moment, and nonjudgmentally to the unfolding of experience moment by moment."[12] When we discuss paying full attention to our immediate experience, it means not only to external forces (*No cheese today*) but all our internal chatter (*This kind of thing always happens to me . . . What idiot failed to order cheese at a burger joint? . . . Why can't I be more mindful and accepting instead of getting angry again?*). We cannot expect to be happy in every situation, but we increase suffering when we fuel our mental fires with self-recrimination (*I shouldn't make such a big deal over a missing dairy product*), rumination (*If only I could stick to vegetarianism, this kind of thing wouldn't happen to me*), prognosticating (*Nothing will ever change*), or any other common tinder.

Being open and curious means acknowledging the reality of the moment, however we feel, without wrestling so much with whatever we cannot affect. Equanimity, a sense of peace and ease, often follows. It's like a secular version of the traditional serenity prayer: We aim to develop for ourselves the ability to change the things we can change, to accept the things we cannot, and the wisdom always to see the difference.

Mindfulness means far more than "Don't sweat the small stuff." It's not twisting ourselves in a knot pretending we're okay when we're not okay. We notice whatever has us rattled without getting so annoyed and blindly reactive. That's because as long as we're caught up in reactivity, unhappiness, frustration, denial, and pushing away from reality as it really is (*Cheeseburger cheeseburger cheeseburger, can't stop thinking about cheeseburgers*), we're not seeing our experience clearly. When we can learn to settle ourselves, time and time again, mindfulness lets us guide ourselves through life's challenges with more clarity and intention.

Sometimes mindfulness reveals details we've hidden from that are quite upsetting but need our attention. *This sucks—I wish his school would stop pushing me to switch his classroom* may seem like a clear statement of reality but probably doesn't help to move you forward. But *I wish my child didn't have a learning disability. I'm scared for him and what it means to be in special education, but I need to do something about his reading* begins to get you somewhere.

With mindfulness, we see things exactly as they are and remind ourselves what we're meant to be doing. We build an ability to live life more fully aware of what's going on both around us and in our mind. Through that awareness, we become more familiar with our ongoing mental habits. That awareness increases our ability to pick and choose (without expecting total success) which habits to continue and which ones might be better to avoid.

We also cultivate a trait of responsiveness over reactivity. With that, we create a little space between our experience (*no cheese*) and whatever we elect to do next. Or maybe for once we allow ourselves to do or say nothing at all, dropping any rumination, plan, or compulsion to fix everything: *I'm disappointed, but I don't have time to go elsewhere. What else can I order today?*

Putting our existence under a microscope is not the goal. That would exhaust anyone. We instead balance a gentle focus with a measure of acceptance. We recognize our own cognitive tendencies without self-abuse. We cultivate a sense of compassion for ourselves and others, a recognition that we're all trying to find some peace and happiness in life, even when we appear to be making a mess of it.

To summarize, mindfulness is a way to care for our brain the same way we care for our body. It's also an accessible, proven way to take care of ourselves while building skills that make life easier to manage—for both ourselves and our children.

Consider This

Aim for mindfulness in everyday life. When you're
with your children, notice when you're distracted and
your attention wanders. Then guide it back to the
full experience of your time together—sights, sounds,
sensations, smells, thoughts, or emotions—in an unforced
way, bringing your attention to your family time.

Mindfulness Starts with You

ONCE PEOPLE SEE the benefits of mindfulness, they often urge spouses, friends, and children to join. But you can't force anyone else into mindfulness. In fact, it's a quick way to turn them off: *You're all wound up. You should meditate more.* The most common way to get someone on board is when they see you benefiting yourself. In other words, if you practice mindfulness as a parent, you've already put your children on the same path.

Kids are sponges that absorb the details of life around them. Treat family, friends, and strangers with warmth, and your child will more likely do the same. Children discover their own habits and go off in their own directions eventually, but their foundation starts at home.

Scientists debate the existence of brain pathways called "mirror neurons."[13] Potentially, these same neurons may fire both when we do a task and when we watch someone else. I drink a glass of water, the nerves fire . . . but if I watch you drink water, they also fire.

In one study, a chimpanzee and a toddler encountered a puzzle box that required a trick to open: moving various parts in the right order. After several trials, an adult demonstrated several steps needed to solve the puzzle, but only the last one mattered. Watching, it was obvious that everything could be skipped, except opening a latch.[14]

The chimpanzee figured it out right away and did only the last step. The child meticulously copied the adult's behavior, going through multiple steps and taking the long way. The initial conclusion? Chimpanzees are smarter than toddlers. After further thought, though, this is what turns out to be true: Kids are driven to copy exactly human adults. This type of response could explain much about how children learn, and perhaps even abstract concepts such as empathy. Mysteries like why a yawn appears contagious or why some people are rabid sports fans may be clarified because of mirror neurons. Watching a favorite player may directly excite the fan's brain at home. For a parent, the idea of mirror neurons suggests how concretely children observe adults in their environment.

Whether or not mirror neurons literally exist—there is much skepticism—the concept holds fast. Kids are hardwired to learn from adults. Because of that, mindfulness is not the kind of thing where, wrapped up on your smartphone, screaming at a co-worker, and giving little attention to the world around you, you can say, "Hey, kid, go meditate." You won't get far telling them to do something you're not doing yourself. But they *will* learn every time they watch you manage a situation in some new way.

To teach children tennis, you play tennis. You don't have to be a star, but you do have to know enough to stay ahead. You'll approach it differently with a teen than a kindergartener. You'll make it fun and unique based on your own judgment and relationships. Teaching anything requires pulling from your own experience and then making it engaging and real.

Mindfulness is no different. As you experiment with various approaches, they become familiar, as with a sport. Like any teacher, you'll adapt, make mindfulness playful when you can, and explain concepts in age-appropriate language. There's no great mystery if you understand mindfulness yourself.

So don't worry about *making* your kids practice mindfulness. If they're intrigued, they will join you. When they're ready, share mindfulness books or use mindful phone apps geared at kids. Overall, though, you'll get further by patiently practicing yourself rather than making it another thing they must do. When they're ready, you'll know, and they will start practicing too.

How we typically discuss mindfulness varies by age. Following are ways kids often grasp the concept of mindfulness and how you can begin to incorporate it at different developmental stages:

Teenagers understand mindfulness much like an adult, and they can follow along with formal meditation practices meant for adults. The key differences relate to language and brain development, adapting concepts to age and life experience. In other words, make it real.

Elementary school and middle school students require a simplified approach to both the ideas around mindfulness and the practices. Attention or listening to sounds, for example, may be entirely understandable. The idea that "thoughts are just thoughts" may initially be too abstract. Meditation practices are shortened, and in younger children an emphasis on movement-based practices can be particularly useful. An easy way to introduce mindfulness in this age range is by making it part of the bedtime routine.

Preschool and early elementary school-age children, once again, largely learn through play. Many mindfulness-related traits develop through play itself, such as impulse control. Others, like emotional awareness, can be built through reading books. But mindfulness practices are possible too, such as asking a child to rock to sleep a stuffed animal placed on their belly and therefore aiding them in focusing on the sensation of their body and breathing.

Consider This

As with any subject, your own familiarity with mindfulness provides everything you need to teach children. Countless apps, books, and programs are available. When it's time, find one that fits how your family approaches life. And if your kids don't want to hear it from you, that's fine too. Come back to your own practice, because mindfulness in your family starts with you.

O IS FOR OLD-FASHIONED EDUCATION

EF Starts with Consistency, Consistency, Consistency

THERE'S AN OLD FABLE that goes something like this: A king wants to know the meaning of life. He hears of a wise man who lives in a tree in the mountains, several days of difficult hiking away. The king seeks him out and asks, "What is the meaning of life?"

The old man in the tree considers deeply, then says, "Treat people as you wish to be treated, work hard, and have fun."

The king says, "That's it? A four-year-old knows that."

And the old man says, "Easy at four. Not so easy at forty."

When it comes to healthy living, you know much of what you need to know already. Life becomes chaotic and gets in the way. Exactly how we would advise our best friend isn't what we choose ourselves. From eating, to exercise, to sleep, to prioritizing family time, early childhood habits become adult habits. Easy to know at four, hard to live it at forty.

Executive function builds from consistent daily routines. For starters, skills involved with organization, planning, and prioritizing develop in this way. Of course, those details may be the first to get lost when life gets busy and pressured.

While kids wait for their brain manager to mature, adults educate through establishing healthy lifestyles. It takes a lot of executive function *not* to eat a favorite junk food every time you see it. Or go to bed at a reasonable time even though it would be fun to stay up late on a school night. Or exercise regularly. It's an ongoing challenge that requires adult-level problem-solving and prioritization.

When we step outside the stress of daily life, some answers are not so complicated. Children learn from experience more than discussion.

If you want your child to eat healthfully, eat healthfully. Try explaining to a toddler he needs to eat his broccoli, though Daddy won't eat it himself. You'll quickly find, as the vegetables fly across the room, that even a sixteen-month-old sees the contradiction. Similarly, the impact of early school start times on high school students' sleep, and therefore attention through the day, seems clear but isn't talked about much. Common-sense solutions are easily missed both by individuals and communities.

The simplest path for children is when something becomes part of the fabric of everyday life that might otherwise be a challenge. Of course you brush your teeth, and of course you exercise, and of course you get your homework done at a reasonable hour. Of course you treat me with respect, and your friends, and everyone else you meet. Why discuss it? It's how we live.

Habits are hard, though. Think for a moment about nutrition. Having a child is a great opportunity to reassess, because, well, you do the shopping. Undoubtedly, some foods feel comforting and enjoyable because they are familiar, but what would you rather your children learn to enjoy? It's hard to change, as we battle our sweet tooth or love of butter and cream, yet our habits spill over onto our families.

Most habits feel permanent even when they aren't. To remain efficient, our minds stop thinking about particular situations—that's how it's done, no need for debate. This is great for something like tying our shoes, not so much when we're having the same useless discussion about homework for the sixteenth time. For any routine, assumption, or habit we've developed as a parent, there's always room to pause and reconsider. Most of us know the basics: Eat well, exercise, avoid stress. Wouldn't life be easier if we had learned something different as a kid?

Recognizing the value of consistency should not become an opportunity to thrash yourself for being inconsistent. We all have challenges that we wrestle with seemingly forever. Children raised in happy homes can grow up sad; those raised in sad homes can grow up happy, and everywhere in between. Your kids will find their own path, likely quite different than yours, in the end—for better or worse. We can only try to give them every chance to succeed in whatever they set out to do.

Like any parenting advice, take everything you read about kids with a grain of salt—or even better, a sense of humor. It's useful to realize that childhood habits grow into adult habits, but none of us lives a perfect life. It's impossible to get anything exactly "right," whatever that is. Parenting is messy and unpredictable.

Instead of creating another debilitating image of family perfection, pick one routine you think worth the effort, and start there. Without judging yourself, what are you modeling when stressed? How do you talk to family members, friends, or other people? What eating habits, exercise routines, and media choices are your children observing? If there's one new habit that might benefit your children, do your best to make that change. Forgive yourself for the rest.

Breaking habits takes persistence and patience. We take a step, we get stressed, we fall back on old routines, and we start again. What are the ABCDs of successful habit formation?

> **A = Assess your motivation.** Start with clarifying why you want a change. *My doctor said* doesn't necessarily hold water. *I'd like my child to grow up healthier than I did* might. Set aside subtle thoughts that intrude, along the lines of *Sounds great, but I always break down; it will never really work.* If there's practical truth to that thought, it's find to acknowledge it. More often, there's no fact to that inner sense of "I can't do it." It's a self-critical habit. Set that unproductive thought aside like you would unsolicited advice from an untrusted acquaintance.

> **B = Build stepwise, attainable goals.** Break longer-term intentions into incremental, more easily accomplished steps when possible. Success sustains motivation, for both children and adults.

> **C = Create structure and reminders.** New habits require reinforcement until done without thought or effort. Set alarms and create visual reminders. Partner with someone and allow them to prompt you. And when it

makes sense, tie a new habit to something you already do regularly, such as, *Each day before bed, I'll meditate for ten minutes.*

D = Debunk perfectionism. Counterintuitively, for many of us, perfectionism undermines motivation. At the first sign of failure, or when the plan needs adjusting, we give up easier than when we're patient with our progress. The intention to improve and work hard doesn't rely on a self-abusive commitment to be perfect. Allow for mistakes, trial and error, and redirection.

Consider This

Don't take modeling a lifestyle as a crushing responsibility. It increases the odds your child lives a certain way but far from guarantees it. There is a huge genetic effect even around personality and temperament. Most, if not all, developmental conditions (such as attention-deficit/hyperactivity disorder or autism) arise out of genetics, having nothing to do with upbringing. And, of course, we all have our bad days and our bad habits and can only do our best.

Books, the Brain,
and Family Relationships

"NEW PRODUCT BUILDS BETTER BRAINS!" Does that headline grab your attention? As parents, we're under constant pressure to do whatever we can to give our children a leg up. For example, claims are continually made about "educational" software, despite little evidence so far that they have much (if any) benefit. In fact, several large companies have been successfully sued for deceptive advertising.[15] Millions of marketing dollars are spent without much grounding in reality, yet seeding doubt that we're not doing enough.

What "new" product truly does promote brain development? It's old school, but new books come out every week. That may not sound flashy, but more than any other "product," books build language and cognitive abilities. In fact, books are one of the only proven household "interventions" that supports child development. At-risk kids immersed in reading from birth have larger vocabularies and become more likely to succeed in school.[16] Reading promotes language skills and may even improve behavior and executive function.[17] From setting up academic success through building background knowledge (a certain amount of familiarity guides learning with any new topic), books are the answer. Read to kids, read with kids, and let them see you reading.

Getting kids to read begins with carving out a place for books in your home. When your children see *you* reading, have reading as part of bedtime, and have screen limits, they will eventually be more inclined to read for fun too. In fact, not enjoying reading can be a red flag for learning disabilities or attention problems. Children who read well will read, given the chance.

Books aren't only about language and learning; they also build social connection.[18] Read together until your child no longer cares to read together (which if you find the right books may be far older than you imagine). Even if reading has never been part of your own life, for the sake of your children, make room in your life for books.

As for the competition in the other corner, the verdict is in: Computers and satellite learning are no substitute for face-to-face education. Not only does "educational" media usually not work, but in one study, infants exposed to educational DVDs actually fell behind peers in language development.[19] Learning and language rely on human interaction, particularly around spoken language and reading. Involved parents and teachers are crucial to child development at home and in the classroom.

Technology is a tool for teachers to utilize but hasn't been shown particularly effective as a stand-alone. It may be entertaining for students to add computers to classrooms. So would providing a bowl of candy. For many children with immature EF, technology becomes an engaging distraction. Computers require active teachers who use them well and show students how to use them wisely too.

In the end, teaching kids requires an engaged, proactive human being. Add a teacher to a classroom and kids will probably progress far more than through an educational game. Someday, a specific product may prove to educate well, and there are many useful online sites, such as the Kahn Academy (kahnacademy.org), that *augment* academics for an engaged student. And still, skilled teachers drive classroom learning far more than a laptop.

For many children, reading time itself relies on parental screen management. Since adult screen habits develop early, and built-in marketing highly influences how children choose to live, more device time frequently pulls from healthier pastimes like reading. The easy, quick path to entertainment is a screen. If you teach a child to depend on screens at the first sign of fussiness and boredom, that pattern continues. Only by shoving technology to the side can we emphasize reading, open-ended play, outdoor play, and family time. Each, in their own way, require some motivation and mental effort.

Less is far more when it comes to promoting development. Without spending any money, without signing up for any classes, any family can set their children up for success. A stable household, clear limits, lots of adult talk, lots of play, and lots of books—these are the things most proven to set children up academically. Take special effort to bring books into your home, emphasize reading as a joint activity, and make reading fun.

Here are some tips adapted from the nonprofit Reach Out and Read for building a relationship with books:

Make reading part of every day. Include it at bedtime as together time for winding down. Even older children can enjoy books you set aside to read together. Encourage independent reading through this trick: Tell children lights out is at a certain time . . . or they can read on their own for fifteen minutes.

Make sure your kids see you reading actual books. For your kids to value reading, you'll need to value reading. As noted earlier, if you use a device for reading, consider switching to real books; otherwise, how can they know you're not playing games yourself?

Make the story come alive. Talk about the pictures. Create voices for the story characters. Elaborate and make jokes. Ask questions about the story. What do you think will happen next? Let your child ask questions, and discuss familiar activities and objects. Make reading an interactive, entertaining event.

Choose books about events in your child's life. Find books about starting preschool, going to the dentist, getting a new pet, moving to a new home, topics or hobbies of interest, or anything that helps a child relate.

Create book time with nonreaders. If someone you know cannot read, encourage them to share books through activities such as describing the pictures and prompting children to do the same.

Books build brains. People build brains. Screens do not build brains. Lots of people are going to try to sell you cutting-edge stuff. No one is going to spend millions of dollars to convince you that the most important product for your child is a pile of books.

> ### Consider This

> A free library card does as much for your child's early development as anything you can buy. Visit your local library often—no need to spend money on this brain-building product at all! Make a weekly trip, keeping a pile of books at home to explore. Each time the pile has been used up ... start again.

Building a Better Learner

MANY EDUCATIONAL TRENDS today put children at a disadvantage. Skewed expectations start in kindergarten, with academic tasks assigned beyond the developmental level of an average five-year-old who cannot sit and attend for very long. Fourth-grade classrooms seem to require what used to be a sixth-grade level of self-regulation and planning, and so on all the way through high school. From classroom design to teaching methods, schools place huge demands on students in ways that for many do not add up.

Classroom setup itself impacts learning. Class sizes have generally gotten larger, though some studies found that smaller ones boost achievement.[20] Desk layout is now often in small clusters, even though most of us find it easier to attend when directly facing a teacher instead of a best friend. Unsurprisingly, desk clusters may lead to distractibility and off-task behaviors.[21] It doesn't take any out-of-the-box thinking to realize that small, well-designed classrooms help children learn.

Newer teaching methods often emphasize self-guided and problem-based explorations (also called discovery-based learning), instead of the direct instruction and reinforcement that most young children require. As stated in the journal *American Educator*, "while experts often thrive without much guidance, nearly everyone else thrives when provided with full, explicit instructional guidance (and should not be asked to discover any essential content or skills). Decades of research clearly demonstrate that for novices (comprising virtually all students), direct, explicit instruction is more effective and more efficient than partial guidance."[22] Most of us benefit from specific direction when learning a new skill, but modern approaches often ask children to figure out academics for themselves.

If you ask experts in almost any field, they recommend starting with the building blocks before moving on to advanced skills. You can't play a Mozart sonata without first studying the scales. Around any new topic, evidence-based teaching relies on sustained instruction, such as explicit guidance around letters and letter sounds required for reading. Learning a skill—from playing piano or baseball to reading and math—requires a solid foundation around the basics.

What does this modern discovery-based trend look like? Silent reading time is emphasized over reading with an adult. For someone with limited reading ability, there is an unrealistic expectation that they will focus, behave, and be productive on their own. Similarly, children are asked to write independently without supports, like using an outline to help organize their thoughts. In math, without placing emphasis on facts and formulas, young children are asked to do things like solve multistep word problems and explain their work in writing, activities that again rely on mature EF.

These newer trends in education also counter much of what we've learned about executive function. EF is the backbone of problem-based learning, approaching new situations, and flexible thinking. Demands on executive function go up whenever students face anything unfamiliar. But without an emphasis on basic concepts and routines, nearly *everything* remains unfamiliar. Academics march forward without students having mastered the information because teachers overestimate the independent learning skills of the average student.

Evidence-based approaches to teaching emphasize feedback, correction, and adult reinforcement of skills until concepts are mastered around any topic. Because a different part of the brain supports fluently learned skills, stressing the fundamentals reduces demands on EF. It may seem instinctual to teach this way, but these proven techniques are out of fashion. If every classroom in the country utilized evidence-based instruction, the result would be a drastic decrease in the number of struggling kids. Teachers almost universally lament the lack of fundamental skills across topics like spelling and math. In reading alone, traditional approaches have over a 90 percent success rate, while newer programs sit near 50 percent.[23] To develop expertise, children require repetition, routine, and solid academic footing. Instead of grasping for flashy answers, sticking with what we know works usually improves education.

Beginning learners go further when taught the basics, instead of figuring them out themselves. Thankfully, many students are resilient enough to learn from any engaged teacher. If your child struggles, regardless of school policy, come back to direct teaching. Ask for it from your school, provide it yourself when you are able, or utilize tutors if you can. From reading, writing, or math, to daily routines or even a sport, let go of educational trends and emphasize the fundamentals to set your child up for success.

> ### Consider This

Long-term success relies on a fluent, accessible foundation across almost every life skill. New teaching techniques should be integrated once shown useful, but nothing replaces small classrooms, well-trained teachers, and proven techniques. Back to the basics means direct teaching from an adult and repetition until skills become fluid and instinctual.

U IS FOR UNDERSTANDING WHEN TO INTERVENE AROUND DEVELOPMENTAL DELAYS

Making the Choice for Intervention

EARLY INTERVENTION MATTERS around any childhood delay. The sooner we step in and offer support, the sooner a child catches up. Yet both parents and pediatricians often put off developmental services. How can parents know when to seek evaluation with a professional?

The tendency to watch and wait makes sense on the surface because it offers children an opportunity to mature. Kids sometimes outgrow early differences. Moreover, not every child develops at the same pace. It's also scary when a child may have a delay—and not uncommon when a parent worries that they are at fault.

The fear of labeling children with a diagnosis that may keep them constricted in a box of lowered expectations frequently keeps families from seeking services. Meanwhile, less supportive labels like "difficult" or "unmotivated" may get used behind the scenes. A diagnosis shifts everyone to the same less-judgmental page, for example, by clarifying that a child has ADHD rather than "he's a handful." An accurate diagnosis also guides intervention, as schools cannot know what a child requires otherwise.

The reality is twofold around child development: Delays are common, with up to one in five kids falling behind in at least one area of development.[24] And most interventions are behavioral and educational, with little downside. A child who acts out will benefit from positively framed supportive measures, regardless of the underlying cause. On the other hand, delayed services compound challenges. For example, falling behind in language often leads to behavioral outbursts; kids may simply not be able to "use their words," as adults endlessly advise. Struggling socially or academically affects self-esteem. For those behind in EF, having a delayed brain manager gets in the way of almost every aspect of life—school, social, behavioral, sports, and even health and safety.

Several options exist for developmental care in most communities:

- Start with your primary care pediatrician.

- Below age three, early intervention programs, provided under the federal Individuals with Disabilities Education Act, offer free evaluation and services.

- Between ages three to five, state committees on preschool special education provide similar services, sometimes in a school-based program and sometimes at home.

- Age five years and older, state committees on special education take over developmental evaluation and care with most interventions occurring at school.

- Professionals offer support through fields such as developmental pediatrics, psychology, speech-language therapy, or tutoring.

What does typical development look like? Informal assessment of child development is never a substitute for structured screening by a professional. The American Academy of Pediatrics (AAP) recommends pediatricians use validated screening tools three times by age three.[25] The AAP's Bright Futures program offers the following guidelines of select milestones to help you recognize concerns that may stand out:

> **One year.** Stands alone, walks (fifteen months); bangs two blocks, scribbles (fifteen months); babbles, says first word; responds to name, waves and points to communicate, shares interests with parent; interactive in play, imitates others

> **Two years.** Throws a ball, jumps, walks upstairs; towers four to six cubes; combines words, knows fifty-plus

words, points to pictures, follows simple requests (by two and a half years); starts to remove/put on clothes; imaginative play (by fifteen to eighteen months), parallel play with peers

Three years. Balances on one foot, wiggles thumb, copies a vertical line drawn by an adult, towers six to eight cubes; speech moves towards 100 percent intelligible, uses sentences and sustains back-and-forth conversation; names a color, names a friend; brushes teeth with help; plays more interactively

Four years. Hops, balances longer on each foot; draws a three-part person (eyes, mouth, head), towers eight cubes; conversational, names colors; copies a cross and circle; engages in imaginative, language-based play with peers

Most of us battle an urge to compare our child's progress to that of their peers. Done without judgment, that comparison might give us a fair sense of a child's development. More often, it's a way to exhaust ourselves with worry. Any time you remain uncertain about your own child's development, instead of waiting and worrying, a good place to start is by checking in with your pediatrician.

> ## Consider This

When a child falls behind, a parent often carries a weight of doubt until they reach out for clarification. You're doing your best—that's what all parents do. If you have worries, or someone you trust raises them, pause and consider. You cannot protect your child from everything, but you can guide them toward resources. You're not doing either of you a favor skirting an anxiety that something is amiss. A developmental evaluation is never a judgment of you or your child.

Nothing More or Less
Than an EF Deficiency

IT'S IMPOSSIBLE to talk about the benefits of executive function with-out touching on attention-deficit/hyperactivity disorder, as ADHD illustrates the opposite side of the coin. That's because, practically speaking, ADHD is a developmental delay of executive function.

Research around ADHD shows consistent differences in parts of the brain responsible for executive function (though not in a way usable for diagnosis yet). The genetics of ADHD alone are as strong as height—just like tall parents will likely produce tall offspring. Put a child up for adoption and the risk of ADHD relates most to her *biological* parents. And in spite of endlessly empty suggestions, the occurrence of ADHD around the world stays near one in twenty, and typically slightly higher, in every country studied.[26]

Beyond misleading and eye-catching headlines, ADHD is a medi-cal condition no different than asthma or eczema, and is not caused by bad parenting or our crazy modern lifestyle. Understanding this larger picture of ADHD can guide any parent toward a better sense of the role of executive function in everyday life.

The starting point for ADHD care is that it is real and impacts EF (and this includes ADD, or attention deficit disorder, now more accurately labeled ADHD with predominantly inattentive symptoms). When parents, teachers, or kids believe ADHD is fake or caused by lack of effort, motivation, or self-control, everyone ends up frustrated and confused. Children wrestling with their own neurology end up without the proper guidance and interventions that allow for catch-up.

ADHD must be handled no differently than any other medical condition—no one wants it, but it is there. Yet ADHD can be hard to recognize, and even suffering school grades aren't the bottom line. There is no one test. Only meticulous history taking and an evaluation seeking persistent patterns around EF development can lead to a diagnosis.

Once a child is diagnosed, families must see ADHD through the context of EF to manage it completely. ADHD has long outgrown its name. Its stereotypical symptoms—lack of attention, hyperactivity, and impulsiveness—merely scratch the surface. It affects anything related to EF—time management, judgment, organization, goal seeking, emotional regulation, social behavior, and even overall stress.

It's difficult for parents, it's difficult for kids, but ADHD isn't anyone's fault. When parents and teachers lose track of that, kids get blamed for behaviors and choices not fully under their control. Apparent misbehavior or even what seems like poor motivation typically come down to skill-based difficulties with focus, staying on task, emotion, or anything else involved in executive function. Parents get falsely blamed by others, or blame themselves too.

Just as some people can draw, shoot a basketball, or play an instrument more easily than others, innate abilities such as planning, remembering, and paying attention are driven by genetics. Chronic forgetfulness, poor preparation, leaving homework assignments behind, not listening when called, throwing tantrums, or giving up too easily . . . all reflect immature executive function. You might choose to teach someone how to shoot a free throw or keep a to-do list in a new way, but the skill will not materialize out of thin air. That's the heart of ADHD care.

When under-addressed, ADHD demonstrates the downside to EF deficiency. It isn't only a school problem. ADHD often causes social and communication difficulties that impact friends, families, and marriages. Accident risks rise from the playground to driving a car. ADHD relates to health conditions such as obesity. Without a strong brain manager, almost any part of life may suffer.

You wouldn't say to a child with asthma, "Just try harder, stop wheezing." Likewise, expecting a child with poor executive function to "pull it together" is unfair and unrealistic. Children require a compassionate and objective view of their abilities connected to long-term plans that offer concrete skills and strategies. We encourage appropriate behavior and hard work while aware that ADHD-related hurdles may get in the way.

When we start to understand the full reality of the situation—that someone with ADHD has a medical disorder affecting how they manage life—we make skillful choices about how we parent, teach, and more. When we recognize the cause of ADHD and its far-reaching symptoms, we shift our short-term expectations while offering intelligent plans that make certain all children with ADHD reach their full potential.

Perhaps the most concise one-line description of ADHD ever is that "ADHD involves more a disorder of performance than of skills; of not doing what one knows more than of not knowing what to do (ignorance)."[27] Most anyone with ADHD knows exactly what they *should* be doing, but they lack the skills to get it done. Solutions arise from seeing ADHD as it is, a frustrating, wide-ranging disorder effectively managed when we realize its impact on executive function. With clear-sighted, comprehensive care, children with ADHD thrive.

> ## Consider This

There is so much stigma attached to the diagnosis of ADHD, when it is in reality a specific delay in a particular skill set. Seeking an evaluation is a vital step for parents and teachers. Knowing if a child has executive function delays changes many things, even before discussion of treating and managing ADHD begins.

Facts Are Facts,
Even Around Child Development

YOU MAY BE FAMILIAR with the story of four blind men who encounter an elephant. One grasps the trunk and says, "I've found a snake." Another presses the side and declares, "We've come to a wall." One grabs a leg and says, "Not at all. It's a tree." The last one touches its tail and says, "There's a rope."

So it is with child development. While alternative options and trends like the ones listed later in this chapter may sound appealing, it is crucial to ask ourselves if they are grounded in evidence, as well as if they are right for our family. Every few years something new arrives, some claim or product throwing forth a new unproven technique. These fads often divert families from more proven, evidence-based ideas. Parents may waste precious energy and money through these diversions instead of sticking to what we already know to be true.

There is basic science, from which we make informed choices. Flip a coin enough times and roughly half the tosses will come up heads. Drop something heavy on earth and it falls instead of rises. If we want to move building material onto a roof, we can't just drop it and cross our fingers that it flies. Quality science has a factual basis and informs our lives.

The same applies in child development. We can remain open to new concepts while also keeping track of what we know. An entrenched idea could be wrong, yet it's equally true that theories spread virally can distract and confuse. Instead of making life easier, they frequently add more to worry about. As if learning disabilities and developmental delays aren't enough, now we must monitor a child's "information processing," vaccines, and nutrition with an overwhelming level of detail.

Western medicine doesn't know everything. When seeking answers, some of us try alternative care, and many complementary interventions show benefit. Here are four basic questions to ask when seeking trustworthy information about alternative options:

1. **Is it safe?** A surprising number of alternative options are risky for children's health. Even a dietary supplement taken to excess can cause illness.

2. **Is it affordable?** Many unproven options are quite expensive and unnecessarily strain families.

3. **Does the theory make sense?** We know a lot about child development and brain science. Something that sounds far-fetched on the surface may be nothing more than far-fetched. Hyperbaric oxygen treatment has been suggested for autism. Why would that ever affect a child's development?

4. **What does the research already say?** Alternative care is well and good, except when done in blind exclusion of what we know. Ample evidence exists that when it comes to much of what worries parents lately, there's nothing to fear.

Beyond opinion, mine or anyone else's, there's reality. You'll find plenty on the Internet and in bestselling books that states otherwise. But studies show that medical information you find on the Internet is rarely accurate, complete, or relevant.[28] The following list sets the record straight on things modern parents needn't worry about:

Crawling. Because of the front-to-back sleeping campaign, infants spend most of their time on their backs. As a result, some skip crawling. If overall development progresses appropriately, and a pediatrician's physical examination is normal, there's no reason for concern if your child skips crawling.

Educational software and DVDs. As noted earlier, large companies have been successfully sued for false marketing around so-called educational media. There's nothing wrong with supplemental academic programs or informative shows, but you can't rely on them to boost academics or cognitive development. One known exception is for children *behind* in preschool language; their vocabulary may expand through PBS-style programming.

Learning styles. Children learn from strong teachers using evidence-based techniques. While children may learn more easily through one modality (visual versus auditory, for example), the fact that children prefer one should be considered a preference, not a requirement.[29]

Nutritional interventions. Apart from poor health, serious deficiencies or proven allergies, cognitive development isn't influenced greatly by diet. Not only that, odd diets are expensive and stressful, frequently eliminating foods kids prefer. The intensity can even harm; for example, overly limiting infant food exposure increases the risk of allergy. Some food dyes may impact behavior, but avoiding neon-colored products isn't that radical a choice. Don't feel pressured toward anything more than a balanced, well-rounded diet.

"Processing" disorders. There's no good evidence that processing disorders exist on their own. *Symptoms* related to processing are *symptoms* of something else. Children with "auditory processing" issues typically have language or attention problems. Part of EF is managing and therefore "processing" what information we encounter through the day.[30] Address the underlying causes first; auditory processing programs are ineffective on their own.[31] Similarly, "sensory processing" issues relate to other developmental disorders (such as anxiety, ADHD, or autism), and sensory interventions benefit most when supplemented with more proven care, like behavioral therapy.[32] Visual therapy has been disproven around academics.[33] Apart from a child being unable to see the page or whiteboards, there is no known link between vision and learning disorders. Anxieties around processing disorders fan empty fears. Proven solutions relate to more well-defined conditions.

Shortcuts to better executive function. A computer-based executive function program makes sense in theory, requiring sustained attention and other EF-based skills instead of the fast-paced, disjointed focus that makes the average video game fun. So does neurofeedback, in which children influence brain function through video game play or similar tasks. Disappointingly, skills gained through these activities so far do not appear to generalize well into real life. To date, mindfulness is the training in both attention and EF that most appears to affect everyday life.

Vaccines. Vaccines have been studied extensively by many, many methods. Add a vaccine to a large population and the incidence of developmental delays does not increase; remove one and it does not decrease. Track children from birth and nothing around development relates to vaccine timing. Children with autism frequently lose skills as toddlers—with or without receiving vaccines. For any vaccine available now, a preventable disease is prevented without a known risk to child development.[34]

Consider This

One challenging but straightforward way to feel less stress is to disregard the trends that have little or no substance. From overly academic preschools to radical diets to the endless marketing onslaught around "educational" products, let them go. Move beyond the message that there is yet one more thing to fear or fix and you'll find a more stable, manageable lifestyle.

Y IS FOR WHY WE WORK HARD

Grit, Mindset, and
Their Relationship to EF

YOUR CHILDREN AREN'T always going to be successful. They aren't going to go through life without ever getting hurt, frustrated, or disappointed. They aren't going to solve every problem on the first try and pick up every skill without effort. And that's perfect.

In classic studies by psychologist and author Carol S. Dweck, PhD, two groups of children were presented with increasingly difficult puzzles.[35] As they progressed, one group received feedback along the lines of "You're doing great, you must be very smart." Another group received praise targeted on effort: "You're doing great, look how hard you're working." What Dr. Dweck found, and later described with the term *mindset*,[36] is that children who are guided toward more fixed traits, like intelligence, don't persist as long. When things get challenging, the internal message becomes, *Well, I guess I'm not smart enough anymore.* In the study, children not only gave up sooner but, left to play on their own, stuck with easier puzzles. Children praised for effort worked harder, and did better—they cultivated a "growth mindset." Even during downtime, those who valued effort pushed themselves with harder puzzles.

Another psychologist and author, Angela Duckworth, PhD, has studied a related concept and calls it "grit."[37] What allows some people to persist when things get tough while others give up? Her research results are similar. When effort is emphasized, children are more likely to persist.

A fixed trait is either there or it is not; if a child fails, there is nothing in their control that they can address to improve themselves. Fixed goals are similar. If the only successful outcome is a perfect grade, winning, or being smarter than the rest, kids tend not to work as hard over time. If only straight As are okay, it's a major failure not to get them. When we teach children to connect hard work to manageable goals, they develop the capacity and desire to sustain effort and become that much more likely to thrive.

Children are smart, so you can't praise effort or successes that aren't there. If you reward effort for utterly bad results, like a carelessly misspelled paper, that on its own doesn't make someone motivated. If you award children for showing up, not actual success and work, they know the scoop. It may undermine hard work if the message becomes *Whatever you do is good enough.*

Interviewed in *The Atlantic*, Dr. Dweck herself has stated that building skills and correcting a child's work are integral to mindset.[38] It's not about empty praise—it's building a perspective. Praise hard work while asking for edits that push learning, and then praise the hard work again (*Look how great that looks now that you've fixed it!*). That's how you show that hard work gets you somewhere.

Focusing on mindset doesn't mean we artificially ignore our children's successes either. It doesn't ruin a child's mindset if we get excited about a grade, award, or winning a game. We're supposed to get excited—we're parents. Mindset means painting in broad strokes, emphasizing hard work and effort: *It's so awesome you guys won—all that practice paid off!*

Growth mindset and grit mean that if you focus on either winning or grades or intelligence alone, children define themselves by those abilities and outcomes. When they hit adversity, they give up when "at first they don't succeed." They limit themselves in perceptual boxes: *I'm not smart enough, or good enough at math, or athletic enough.* When the going gets tough, a step-by-step, hard-work-driven approach to adversity makes long-term success more likely.

Consider This

As with any part of childhood development, mindset and grit start with parents. How do *you* approach adversity? Not only what do you speak about, but what do your children observe? How would they describe your attitude toward hard work, persistence, and problem-solving? Most of us have a growth mindset toward some activities and a fixed approach to others: *I'll never meditate. That's for someone else.* What do your children learn from you day to day?

Motivation in Kids Relies on Success

LET'S SAY YOU want to climb Mount Everest, but you haven't done more than walk to the mailbox in the past few years. As an adult, what do you do? You'd find a training program that slowly builds endurance. You might fail entirely at first. It might even be painful. You can't even walk a mile up a steep hill, and training hurts. You might fail to meet any of your first goals. And then, with an adult brain, you might say to yourself, *Even if I'm only 10 percent successful this week, next week will be twelve, and it will get easier and easier. It's going to hurt along the way, but I'm scaling Everest.* There's little immediate enjoyment or positive feedback, yet you keep your eye on the prize and eventually reach your goal.

Most kids can't do that. In large part because of their EF, kids learn almost entirely from experience. You can't motivate through cajoling, hassling, or discussion. Only an adult thinks, *A year from now I want to climb a huge mountain. Right now I can barely move uphill. It's going to be so satisfying to overcome this pain.*

The Puritan work ethic, that inner drive, well, that's a stereotype. It's a piece of what children require; they *eventually* must value hard work. But motivation requires far more—goal setting, sticking to goals, and skills—to accomplish those goals. The capacity to sustain effort and adapt to challenges requires not only an inner drive but concrete abilities too.

Consider academic motivation. If a child fails a subject, they frequently lack the brain power to create a new plan. It's usually not poor motivation when a child doesn't come up with a solution. Highly motivated, they may not see anything useful to do next. They often cover up with apparent apathy, but all children would rather succeed than not. They may even say, "I guess I should study more," without any idea what that would actually entail.

All the way through high school, the solution starts with adult guidance through the task, establishing a plan and the intermediate steps to accomplish it. Facing a daunting academic hurdle with no apparent solution, kids understandably turn away. If you saw a mountain as an endlessly tall cliff, you'd turn back too. To sustain motivation frequently means parents and teachers schedule extra help sessions, reorganize homework, or do whatever else seems useful up until a time a student shows themselves capable. When those adult-created actions cause a success, kids begin to connect that outcome to effort.

So much of motivation also relies on executive function. Focus, persistence, problem-solving, and long-term thinking, all of that is EF, not motivation in any isolated sense. And as you now know, EF doesn't mature until adulthood. *Feeling* motivated and being *able* to sustain focus toward a goal are not the same concept. Sustained motivation requires both wanting to succeed and the ongoing effort to get somewhere.

Immature EF often looks like poor motivation. The best short-term decision is often *not* to practice piano: *It's sunny and warm and I want to go outside . . . why shouldn't I? A few years from now, I'll be a great piano player, and that will be fun? Forget it. Let's go play.* At an early age, there aren't always visible benefits to the long-term gains of practice.

An adult brain manager ties practice to improvement through supervising the experience. Practice gets scheduled, like brushing teeth. We make sure whatever needs to happen does happen. Over time, piano gets easier and more fun (or maybe we switch to a new activity if piano doesn't seem a good fit). Then we provide more freedom when we observe that a child has developed their own motivation and goal-setting capacities.

Even teens rely on support this way, though they may push back and deny it. Sure, it would be awesome if they could do *it* themselves from the start (whatever "it" you hope they'll overcome this year). With an average adolescent's executive function, they cannot always produce adequate long-sighted decisions or defer gratification well (*My friends are online, but I need to study*). Even for teens, adults sometimes need to lay out what keeps them on track. Self-advocacy is a worthy goal, but it relies on EF.

Motivation requires concrete skills along with the capacity to flexibly problem-solve, focus, and persevere. That means it's our job as parents to:

Encourage skill building. Focus on developing EF and offer direct instruction around other concrete abilities (such as those related to academics or extracurricular activities) when needed.

Set fair expectations. Since goal-oriented behavior relies on EF, keep child development in mind whenever setting intentions.

Create incremental goals. Until a child develops the skills, adults define useful steps toward larger goals.

Acknowledge effort and hard work when you see it. Mindset matters too, as part of a larger, skill-based perspective on motivation.

Consider This

For most children to sustain motivation, adults guide them through a carrot-and-stick approach. Children have a hard time staying engaged without positive feedback and success. It's an exceptional child who persists indefinitely without something going well, whether around reading, writing, baseball, or dance. Breaking larger goals into manageable parts does not lower the bar but instead allows for methodical progress that keeps children engaged.

Persistence + Skill = Resilience

IF ALBERT EINSTEIN had no executive function, we probably wouldn't know his name today. It's well and good to be brilliant, but he also persisted through difficulty, flexibly pushed boundaries of thought, and finished what he started. For all the rumors about him having a learning disability, he didn't get by on brains alone. He managed challenges well too.

Motivation alone doesn't guarantee success. If asked to stand on one leg for the next few hours, you'd make it for a while. If asked to stand on one leg for a million dollars, you'd make it longer . . . and you'd still be limited by your actual physical capacities. Lasting success requires both underlying abilities and motivation, not one or the other.

It's the same for our children when they face adversity. To thrive, they must learn to persevere and develop the actual skills that allow them to handle problems. They need to develop resilience: the capacity to handle challenges and bounce back.

We'll exhaust ourselves and fail when trying to protect our kids from all harms and challenges. The world always throws surprises. Parents make mistakes and will always be far less than perfect. We cannot control or predict the future, but we can provide tools so that our children thrive on their own one day.

Even if you are fortunate enough to have a child without many challenges, focus on long-term resilience. Something will inevitably arise one day, unpredictably and in force, that requires effort and skillful management.

Here are the four cornerstones that together support long-term resilience in both children and parents:

Focus on strengths. While we all have plenty to work on in life, we also have strengths. Home is a great place to begin, starting with positive feedback and praise. From there, resiliency grows as children acquire a clear sense of what they enjoy and what they do well, and they see that their parents value the same.

Cultivate social relationships. As often described by the brilliant psychologist Dr. Robert Brooks, resilience increases when a child grows up around at least one adult providing consistent affection and acting as a role model. For adults, resilience builds from family and friends; for some, it also builds from faith and religion. The US military uses social media in its resilience program, reaffirming a connection with loved ones back home. Family and friends create an irreplaceable platform of emotional support.

Build practical skills. EF represents skills needed to problem-solve, persist, manage emotions, interact with others, and consider the future. Because of that, everything covered in this book supports resilience, from the activities and routines we emphasize as adults to teaching children problem-solving skills, through the practice of mindfulness.

Emphasize a positive attitude toward adversity. People who bounce back easier when stressed see themselves as capable of making a change and value effort and incremental steps forward—this is the role of mindset and grit. Focus on effort while building a belief in competency and an ability to learn and grow.

Consider This

Keep track of the big picture of parenting. All this
information about motivation and executive function
could be used to drive yourself crazy, but it's just
something to try out over time. Once again, don't
aim for perfection. That's not what any discussion of
parenting should suggest.

Part 3

PRACTICAL, POSITIVE PARENTING
Self-Management Every Day

*

How our kids develop and what they need hasn't much changed through the years, even though it may seem like life has become far scarier and more dangerous than when we grew up. You can rest assured (and rest better) learning about what works for most children as they mature toward adulthood. Let's now move onward to everyday living, such as nutrition and sleep, viewed through the lens of executive function, research, and plain old common sense.

Behavior and the Brain: The Early Years
(*I Want It Now*)

HERE IS A TYPICAL child's opinion of ice cream: *I want it. I want it because I see it. I want it when I don't see it too. I want it now, and I want more in ten minutes. Ice cream is good for breakfast and even better for lunch or dinner.*

Depending on your child, the same can be said about video games. Or maybe staying up late. Or not sharing. Or lots and lots of other choices and behaviors that, in the end, just aren't good for them.

Fostering emotional attachment is not an excuse for a child to rule the house. Children are not born with innate self-control; they cultivate this skill. They are impulsive by nature and have no time window linking choices made now to the future. They also do not possess the full ability to defer gratification: *Ice cream tastes good . . . why not eat it all the time?*

A parent's job is to teach through limits while modeling healthy ways to deal with any frustrations that come up in response. When enforced in a positive, loving manner, these limits build self-regulatory skills that foster brain development. Setting clear, understandable boundaries does not need to feel punitive. Through limits, children develop patience and an ability to regulate emotions. Reasonable limits increase the likelihood that children will manage challenges well and live a happy life as an adult.

Here's how young children learn behaviorally in a nutshell: Something happens, and whatever happens next makes it either more or less likely that the behavior is repeated. Discussion with children fosters communication and explains our perspective, but acute behavioral management stems from *immediate* feedback. That's the reality of EF for even the brightest child often all the way into young adulthood.

Discussion is discussion, and discipline is discipline—they aren't the same. Discussion represents a long-term path to collaboration and emotional understanding: "It's disrespectful to hit me. Please don't do it again." First, you take care of discipline, and then when you think it appropriate you explain the "why" of your choices after the fact. Over the years, you share your ideas about how to live. With teens, when possible, you collaborate in decisions while offering them more independence. However, a serious talk isn't always useful discipline even with teens. Influencing behavior *today* means tying whatever happened *now* to whatever happens *next*.

Without the benefit of executive function, young kids cannot fully tie now to the past or future. "Wait till Mommy comes home" doesn't change behavior in a four-year-old. They may seem upset when the punishment finally happens, but it doesn't tie concretely to their earlier misbehavior. Conversely, from elementary school through high school, any student enjoys hearing in the moment, "Great job studying so hard for that test."

Discipline does not only relate to misbehavior or a tantrum—it's a way of modeling healthy relationships. It teaches children to set boundaries on their own behavior, to use language to express anger, and to feel comfortable with intense feelings. When you're compassionate and calm while maintaining appropriate limits, you embody traits your children will, hopefully, emulate themselves.

As close as you may be with your child, you are a parent, not a friend. Adults make decisions, some of which children may not understand. Even when kids have a real reason to complain, *you* should be treated with respect. You make the rules, you uphold them, and that's how children learn.

It may feel simplistic to address behavior so directly, without all the discussion, but it's an honest acknowledgment of the brain. The same model works to encourage a well-behaved child to try new things, like studying extra. Instead of aiming to convince them to work more, set up a reward and reinforce what you want to see. Then, because school gets easier, your child learns from the actual experience.

The ABC model below summarizes how to steer childhood behavior. Adults typically have three places to intervene:

A = Antecedent. Something triggers a behavior; it occurs for a reason: *I want it; I cannot have it.* Or, as another example, an overwhelmed child often misbehaves. When you adjust the difficulty of homework or address her learning disability, the behavior (such as tantrums around schoolwork) often goes away.

B = Behavior. Something is said or done in reaction to that trigger: *I want it, so I'm grabbing the toy.* Perhaps the most important detail about any behavior is that it is far easier to redirect than squash entirely. *Don't yell at me* is harder to accomplish than *When you feel like yelling, go to your room to calm down.* Something motivates the behavior, so doing nothing at all is hard.

C = Consequence. After the behavior, whatever happens next either reinforces or discourages it. *I throw a tantrum; I get the cookie* is one possibility. *I throw a tantrum; I get ignored* makes tantrums far less functional. Since attention is a powerful motivator, ignoring a behavior (not a child, of course) is often as powerful as a punishment.

Encourage behaviors you like, discourage behaviors you don't. No matter how embarrassing and painful it is to deal with tantrums in the short run, no matter how long they persist, the effort pays off. Give in to your child's whining and you reinforce difficult behaviors. You can comfort a child who is upset and angry without changing what you have decided, nudging them that much closer to handling frustration better.

Respond calmly, redirect, but don't give in (*It's okay to be upset but not to act like that*). It is normal for toddlers and young children to test boundaries, to get frustrated, or to cry. Ignore whining, tantrums, and similar behaviors and they disappear quicker—and you have reinforced a message about managing emotions too.

Young brains don't necessarily understand why a behavior is wrong. A child hitting or not treating other kids with respect needs prompt, consistent discipline, limits, or alternatively rewarding the *opposite*, appropriate behavior. Reasoning or rationalizing isn't enough—kids don't stop speaking nasty to peers in the short run just because someone says it makes someone else feel bad. They *gradually* learn from discussion over the years, and open conversation over the years shares your perspective and beliefs about how to live well. Discipline, though, remains *immediate*.

Parents overall have six tools that guide a child's behavior. On the positive side: (1) consistent time together, (2) targeted praise, and (3) focused reward systems. On the corrective side: (4) utilizing time-outs, (5) planned ignoring, and (6) larger consequences (loss of privileges). From intensely difficult behavior to nudging a child toward better time management, return to this basic framework to guide behavior, educating children on the ways of the world.

Here are some other useful tips about limits and discipline to consider:

Steer behavior through immediate feedback. Seek a balance between lovingly meeting a child's needs (*That was great, nice job listening*) but firmly saying no when appropriate (*That wasn't okay at all; please go sit in time-out*). Use verbal feedback to keep kids on track; praise them just before they get distracted or upset and you help them hold themselves together. Whenever possible, pause and insist your child respectfully ask for what they want, even if you've already decided to say yes.

Create opportunities for children to be in control, make choices, explore, and be creative. Creating two acceptable choices allows children to feel a sense of control but still gets you, the parent, what you need. Saying, "Do you want to come inside now or in five minutes?" feels a lot better to both you and your child than "Get inside this instant!" Especially in younger children, that diversion may be enough to "enforce" your decision.

Avoid empty demands. Limit the number of rules when you can, but enforce the ones you choose. If you bend the rules every time your children fuss, it makes sense for them to kick and scream. If they gain twenty more minutes of play while waiting you out, they'll continue playing. Wouldn't you do the same? Children will learn that what you say and what you mean are two different things.

Remain empathetic but firm. Most infants, toddlers, and young children have not yet learned how to express themselves emotionally. They may really, really want to stay downstairs two hours past bedtime and get really, really upset when told to go to bed. Getting upset is normal, healthy even, while learning to manage emotions and frustration. Tell them, "I know you don't want to leave, but we can play again tomorrow. Now it's time for sleep." As long as your child is happy and living in a home full of affection and positive feedback, you are not doing anything wrong if sometimes he gets upset.

Model remaining calm yourself. Show children an appropriate way to respond when frustrated and how to recover when you have a bad moment yourself. Habitual yelling teaches children that yelling is the best response during confrontation; it comes back at you one day. Don't expect perfection of yourself, but do your best and reconnect with honesty about your own behavior (*I wish I hadn't lost my cool—let's talk about what happened*) when you feel the need.

Consider This

A structured behavioral plan will help you stay calm when children push back. It's like the ABC model for adults. First there's a trigger, like your child misbehaves. Instead of falling back on habitual behavior (*I yell to control a situation, or I shut down and give up*), you have a mental checklist to manage the situation (*I'm going to remind her about the reward system, and then fall back on a time-out if that fails*). The consequence leads to a calmer household and well-behaved children—a reinforcement of your own behavior.

Time-Outs in Real Time

WITH SUCH AN OVERLOAD of information on the Internet, there's been growing controversy about how trustworthy certain websites really are, especially around advice on medicine and parenting. Because the Internet is often the go-to source for behavioral issues, a research group set out to see just how reliable online information is for implementing discipline. Every parent needs a firm way to guide behavior. When it comes to time-outs, how safe and effective are they?

For this relatively uncontroversial topic, the research found the web not dependable at all.[1] In fact, the odds of finding "complete and accurate information" were "near zero." Thirty percent of searches falsely suggested that time-outs might be harmful. Inaccuracies, omissions, and inconsistencies were found in all 102 websites explored.

Because of this misinformation, many parents believe time-outs are ineffective and turn to less useful techniques instead. That's a shame, because time-outs are a proven positive parenting tool for enforcing limits—when implemented correctly. They are one of the few disciplinary strategies recommended by the American Academy of Pediatrics to reduce concerns like noncompliance, oppositional behavior, verbal and physical aggression, destruction of property, and temper tantrums. What is more, they cut down on shouting and stress. Here are the go-to guidelines for implementing time-outs, according to the latest research:[2]

> **Time-outs should be a part of positive parenting.** As discipline, time-outs work best when parents also rely on affection and rewards. A high ratio of positive to negative feedback by parents provides a contrast that makes time-outs most effective. This may be the most important message of all from the research.

Time-outs should be served in a boring environment.
The effectiveness of the time-out is impacted by the
amount of activity available to a child. The more
stuff there is—TV, computer, cell phone, toys, even a
coloring book and crayons—the less effective the time-
out. Typically, that means staying in a chair or on a stair.

Use one warning only. Making one brief unemotional
statement (*If you do not do as I say, you will be going
to time-out*) has been found to reduce the number of
time-outs a child will ever go through. By contrast,
repeating the warning decreases the effectiveness of the
punishment (*I'm going to start counting soon; I already
said so once*). Immediacy is equally important. The delay
between the inappropriate behavior and the initiation of
the time-out should be as short as possible to reinforce
your message.

Stick to a reasonable length of time. Time-outs of
moderate length are more effective than shorter ones
and may be as effective as longer ones. A general
recommendation for time-outs is one minute per year of
age. However, some research suggests that a maximum of
four or five minutes is adequate regardless of a child's age.

Don't rely solely on a timer. Waiting to release a child
from time-out until they are quiet and calm (even if the
timer goes off) is more effective in reducing disruptive
behavior than allowing a child to leave when they are
still kicking and screaming.

Be consistent. Pick a few bad behaviors (or even just
one) to target and give your child a time-out every time
they engage in those behaviors. Giving a time-out only
sometimes for the same misbehavior confuses children
and makes learning the rules hard.

Always follow through. Children should not be allowed to escape a time-out by agreeing to obey after you have told them to go to time-out. Once you've stated that a time-out will happen, make it happen.

Make it known who is in charge. And that's you. Evidence suggests time-outs become significantly less effective when a child determines when punishment ends (*Sit there until you are ready to leave*) compared to an adult determining when it is over (*I'll let you know when you can get up*). If your child leaves a time-out before you say to, return them quickly to it (without talking to them much) or provide a back-up consequence, such as no screen time that night.

Get the behavior right in the end. Kids end up in a time-out for doing something wrong or not doing what they're told. Don't let them off the hook. When the time-out is complete, return to the scene of the crime (*Now go back and pick up your toys*). If you don't make closure, the same incident is more likely to be repeated.

> ## Consider This

An emphasis on consistent, immediate feedback when steering a child's behavior doesn't mean being distant or never explaining yourself. Joke around, offer choices, and keep it light even during a moment of discipline, when you're able. When it's time for immediate consequences, stick to them; otherwise, discuss what you think and feel about life, and explain your perspective around rules when that feels appropriate.

Behavior and the Brain: The Teen Years
(*Leave Me Alone . . . Except When I Need You*)

THE TEEN YEARS HAPPEN. You can't avoid them, and you don't want to anyway. It's exciting to watch your child grow toward adulthood, but also terrifying and often an exasperating mess. Your relationship with your child evolves as you gradually let go and boost them into their future . . . and yet teens will be teens.

Adolescents look more grown up, and sometimes act grown up, but their brains are not yet grown up. EF typically matures in the late twenties. As a bottom line, come back to that simple fact. One reason kids do dumb stuff like sexting and drinking and skipping out on school is they don't have mature EF to do otherwise—long-term thinking, problem-solving, emotional skills, and judgment all have a long way to go. And because of that, they require guidance and an adult influence until they learn better.

As parenting expert Wendy Mogel, PhD, describes in her book *The Blessing of a B Minus*, teens are dopamine machines driven by novelty and excitement.[3] A volatile emotional and hormonal mix courses through their bodies. And their social world becomes paradoxically driven by a fierce desire for independence and an equal one to be accepted by and part of their social pack.

Normal development means that teens push away from parents. They crave—and deserve—an opportunity to explore. Because teens will stumble and make mistakes, a parent's job is to remain involved and create a safe container for exploration (*Sure, go out with your friends Friday night, but be home by midnight*). If all is well, they may never notice your rules, and yet boundaries are clearly required when they do bang into one (*If you don't stick to curfew tomorrow, you're not going out next weekend*). Allow all the freedom a teen is capable of sustaining, but monitor whatever keeps them safe, healthy, and, in the long term, happy.

You have the mature EF. You keep track of the big picture and create parameters that keep teens safe. They naturally push back against those boundaries, but that's fine too. Adolescents require more discussion and a transition to a more collaborative approach with parents. But the bottom-line expectations still get defined by adults about health and safety, respecting others, academic responsibilities, and all the complexities of life.

So sure, let teens take a first crack at solutions. Be flexible—maybe they'll think of something feasible that's different than you pictured. Allow for natural consequences, letting them learn through experience sometimes. When a more concerning pattern arises, step back in and get involved. Provide more prolonged attention and direct guidance, and consider seeking academic or psychological supports—in other words, the perspectives of grown-ups.

Through open discussion, steer a teen toward reasonable choices without dictating exactly what to do at first. Find a place of agreement, and acknowledge a teen's point of view before stating your own (*Sounds like that will be a fun party*). Stay honest and explain your concerns, then stick to your own judgment. Your expectations around their behavior, what is safe, and how you are spoken to educate them about what's appropriate and serve as an ongoing model for parenting as you guide them into adulthood.

As Dr. Mogel also recommends, come back often to "when . . . then" statements: "When I see that you're driving safely, then you can use the car at night" or "When it feels like your grades have started to come up, then you can stop tutoring." These give clear explanations of your expectations and assist your teen toward their goal, if they'll listen.

Build a sense of responsibility and community within your own home. As EF matures, teens are capable of chores, picking up after themselves, and helping out around the house. Create expectations that everyone together chips in and makes the household run well.

How does all of this tie back to raising resilient teens? As discussed in Persistence + Skill = Resilience, children benefit from positive relationships, a focus on effort and incremental goals, a clear sense of their strengths, EF, and other specific skills required to succeed when challenged. (Adult resilience research suggests exactly the same for parents.) These four cornerstones together create a foundation for long-lasting success.

When it comes to EF, skills accumulate through early adulthood. Know your own teen, as some mature more quickly than others. Balance that possibility with a clear sense that most teens need more direct assistance, rules, or limits. Build skills by gradually allowing for more independence, choice, and responsibility. Remember, EF is required for planning, goal setting, and long-term judgment. It's quite easy for social pressure or emotion to swamp better judgment.

The basics of guiding teens will evolve, but they'll stay within the same framework as when teens were younger. There are positive approaches, and there are more corrective ones. Lean on the positive approaches first, and aim for consistency when falling back on the negative ones. Here are some guidelines:

> **Focus on relationships.** They're growing up, but they're still your kids. As long as your teen stays willing, prioritize time together, allowing them to choose what to do. Making time for regular family meals correlates with healthier teen behavior. Teens are also influenced and supported by their friendships in a new way, which may require you to gracefully step back a bit and give them space.

> **Use targeted praise.** Positive feedback and approval guides behavior throughout life. Continue to value effort and incremental goals. Engage with their random explorations, showing that you value their new interests as long as they last. Dr. Mogel likens positive feedback and time together as money in the bank—goodwill to sustain your relationship when it's time for limits or a confrontation.

Allow natural consequences. As children explore their world and build EF, they need more room to find their own way. Allow for mistakes . . . to a point. It's like sailing; small corrections in direction are easy when moving through the wind. When you stop paying attention, larger corrections to your course become more difficult.

Set limits. While waiting around for a grown-up frontal lobe for your child, maintain your limits and sustain expectations. Ease into increasingly more responsibility. Let your child show their capacities, and provide freedom when they're able to take it responsibly. But when needed, step in with a firm consequence. It's okay if your teen is "grounded" or if you set a curfew. In fact, allow your teens to blame you whenever they feel pressured or uncertain socially (*My annoying parents won't let me stay out late*). You're supposed to be a parent. It's understandable that you'll be resented once in a while.

Reinforce rewards systems. Rewards work well at any age. Since teens still learn greatly from experience, external motivation may be required until they more tangibly feel the value of, say, extra studying. Encourage productive behaviors by awarding points for them (*Each day you put in fifteen minutes on your Spanish vocabulary, you earn a point toward those speakers you want*). Teens, more than younger children, can also get negative consequences (*Each time you speak disrespectfully to me, you lose a point*). Just as with younger kids, create incremental goals. Reward plans only work when kids succeed more than fail, so adjust the system itself if that doesn't seem to be happening—and consider whether some particular skill needs work for your child.

❯ Consider This

One subtle way to steer teen behavior harnesses their inherent desire to be independent from the adult world.[4] So much money is aimed at influencing teens. Make "take a stand" a general concept in your household. Tell them to behave a certain way and they may rebel from that adult instruction. But turn a healthy behavior into a statement of independence, and teens will more likely comply. Smoking, for example, can be reframed as a battle against Big Tobacco. Even technology can be repositioned: *If you want to be your own person, don't let the tech firms decide your life. It's all designed to manipulate your behavior and keep you hooked. Are you being used, or are you using technology?*

Lovable and Healthy Nutrition
for Children

FEAR AROUND NUTRITION—whether children appear to eat enough or too much or even the right foods—is a hardwired protective instinct. This concern has been blown to new levels through Internet-driven factoids, making parents feel that catastrophe lurks. We read about a food sensitivity, for instance, unknown for generations until now, and wonder if it might be ruining our child's development. But allergies and sensitivities are rare, and most children do fine within a wide range of healthy eating.

That "range," of course, is defined by parents. We're the ones who shop and set the rules. Kids can't fully monitor what they eat. How could they without mature EF? They can't consistently tie decisions now to the future (either tonight or ten years from now) or control impulses when something looks tasty. They can't consider what they had for lunch in relation to dinner, or figure out the factual implications of drinking soda with meals: Kids generally think, if it looks good and it's here now, they should have some.

There's a modern implication that setting limits around food leads to disordered eating. But parents must create some boundaries. You wouldn't serve nothing but cake all day, and it's okay to ask a child to eat a meal before dessert. Some children monitor themselves better than others, but all children benefit from supervision. Of course they prefer sugar, fat, starches, and junk food—those things taste good. A child's EF must rely on adults to carve out useful eating habits.

It comes down to the basics of behavior: With patience, persistence, and a load of parental willpower, children one day, perhaps months or years down the road, move past limited choices around food, even if they kick and scream and go to bed hungry once or twice while figuring it out. Offer kid-friendly options sometimes, mixing in pizza and mac and cheese and ice cream. Keep it light around food whenever possible, and try not to lock horns over it, but stay in line with your larger views of what's best for growing bodies.

Around food, like with anything else, there's a trigger (*I don't want it*), a behavior (*I throw a tantrum*), and a consequence (*Dad gets angry, but then I get to eat buttered pasta for dinner*) that potentially reinforces the behavior. Another option—*I throw a tantrum then I get hungrier, and then I end up eating whatever was on the table to start*—discourages it. Stay resolute but dispassionate, offer choices when appropriate, but stick to your household routines, all while aiming to diffuse fussy behavior around food.

Giving in to limited palates creates a loop, reinforcing specific behaviors around eating. When a child puts up a fuss and then gets what he prefers, he'll put up a fuss again. Kids don't need Pop-Tarts for breakfast and sauceless pasta for dinner. Continually offer healthy choices (discussed more below) through the years and eventually most kids will like what you serve. Even the pickiest eaters follow the same rule: They won't let themselves starve.

When it comes to nutrition, there's also no need to micromanage. Most kids decide when they're full, even if they need a firm hand guiding them toward balanced choices along the way. They'll do what they want when they're out of the house, and we don't have to be worried about a party or night out at a ball game. But there's a time to say, *Enough ice cream*, or *No more chips*, or *Only fruits or vegetables for snacks today*. Parents remain involved and lead children around food as they would around any habit or behavior in childhood.

Up until your pediatrician says your child is not at an ideal weight, your kids are eating enough. Children typically won't let themselves go hungry, however little it seems they are eating. Vitamin and other nutrient deficiencies are quite rare, and usually products of truly extreme diets. Supplements—giving amounts beyond the typical recommendation—haven't been shown to do much, and can even be dangerous.

The same thinking applies to getting overweight. Some people gain weight easier than others. Yet weight gain happens one pound at a time, and it's easier to never gain than to try to lose weight. Raise active kids, protect them from too much screen time, and feed them a healthy diet—that's what you influence most as a parent.

Decades of nutrition research come down to one consistent suggestion: The healthiest path is a traditional Mediterranean diet. A traditional Western diet is a learned palate full of vacuum-packed bags, red meat, fast foods, butter on everything, and lots of soft drinks. The Mediterranean approach emphasizes fruits and vegetables (not fried); olive oil (over butter); whole grains, legumes, and nuts; and moderate consumption of protein (and seafood more than meat). It's not radical, only different from what's become normal in our lives. It may seem a long way from your community or family preferences, but taking even little steps toward better eating habits matter.

Healthy eating grows out of a healthy lifestyle, whether or not that's how you were raised. For all the arguing over whether fat or sugar or gluten or anything else specifically matters more than anything else, the answer is almost certainly *none of the above*. A well-rounded diet from the start is a lot easier than trying to break entrenched eating habits later.

The echoes of an adult lifestyle start young. For example, various studies let children loose in play supermarkets.[5] The objects on the shelves varied, and researchers tracked which items the children were drawn to. Toddlers whose family members drank or smoked regularly were more likely to pretend to do the same. Similar research shows kids drawn to products they've seen advertised. Marketing works. Studies have shown that children exposed to advertising about unhealthy food products have an increased likelihood of consuming those products.[6] And children who are overweight in preschool are at high risk for obesity as adults.[7]

Check in, without judgment, with your own lifestyle. Do you offer healthy foods at most meals? Do you eat too many desserts or too much junk food? Is regular exercise something your child sees you value? No one is perfect; we all have ruts we've fallen into, but awareness allows for change.

Aim for being firm but not restrictive around food; if dessert and junk food are never available, they become way too important a goal.

Make it an exception, though, not the rule. If you don't have desserts and chips around all the time, they don't become part of a lifestyle. Dessert can be a piece of fruit sometimes, if that's a how a child is raised.

Like much of parenting, there's a vast middle ground around reasonable nutrition. Patiently offer the right foods over time, without pushing them, and the drive to eat what Mommy or Daddy eats wins out. It's generally believed that kids need to be offered a new food on average fifteen to twenty times or even more before they'll try it.[8] Most parents give up after four or five tries. We decide our child may never eat something long before he has drawn the same conclusion.

Beyond the anxiety of wanting your child to eat and grow (which may never fully abate), on a literal level there's nothing more to worry about than finding what works for your family and holding true. Here are some general guidelines to consider:

> **Start with you.** Pause, notice how your shopping habits influence family eating habits, and then decide what you want in your home. Simple to say; hard to do. Our preferences are intense, and our emotional connection to foods date to childhood. Cravings may feel too powerful to redirect. Becoming a parent is an opportunity to pause and reflect on the food environment you want for your children.

> **Stay firm.** Early childhood nutrition is another place where persistent, kind parenting wins. Because kids don't have mature EF, too much freedom around food when they are young creates preferences you'd rather avoid later. Joke around, redirect, praise trying new foods, taste them yourself, keep meals fun whenever possible, but as a bottom line, focus on healthy long-term habits.

> **Manage your own fear.** There's an evolutionary, often irrational, fear that our children will not get enough calories to grow. With that anxiety-fueled trigger, it's

easy to become caught up in getting them to eat anything at all. But the facts remain: With food around, kids will eat. Catch yourself, settle, and whenever possible steer away from tension and arguing over food. Eat well yourself, and resolutely focus on the long-term benefits of a balanced, well-rounded diet.

> ## Consider This

Marketing uniquely influences kids. Billions of dollars are spent every year on advertising and manipulating food to make it almost addictive. Familiarity with a brand name (like a soft drink) makes us more likely to pick it even if we feel we're being totally random. Advocates want to pull ads from video games because they work so well. To disarm that marketing, discuss it. Make a joke of ads, pointing out how desperately they want to influence our behavior. Also, avoid exposure to marketing whenever possible, fast-forwarding or choosing ad-free options.

To Sleep, Perchance to Sleep

IT'S 7:30 P.M. and you hand-hold your preschooler to bed, give him a kiss, turn down the light, and crack the door just enough to alleviate his aloneness. But how long before he's at your knees begging because he cannot sleep or wants a drink of water for what seems like the ten thousandth night in a row? You blow him another kiss and wish him a good night's sleep—for his sake, you say to yourself, but in reality also for your own.

Most every parent has experienced the claustrophobic dread that takes over the room while trying to convince a child to lie down, close his eyes, and stay still long enough to fall asleep. We console and cajole, we beg and plead, but he is not at all compelled to hear about the importance of good sleep for his health and happiness tomorrow.

The impact of disrupted sleep can be extensive. It can have deleterious effects on cognitive development, mood, and the ability to pay attention and behave. Studies show it may even impact parental health and well-being, as an infant or toddler who cannot sleep through the night is a potential cause of maternal depression.[9]

There's no doubt about it: Bedtime epitomizes all the demands and challenges inherent to parenting. Our children don't have the EF skills to be wise and long-sighted: *While I want to play and want my mommy, we'll both feel better after a good night's sleep. I'll run upstairs and tuck myself in.*

Around each chaotic bedtime, we (hopefully) remain calm on the outside, churn on the inside, and muster our resources only to discover, when nightfall calls, that once again we cannot control everything after all. Yet evidence also tells us that getting our little ones, even infants, to fall asleep by themselves and rest through the night is more than wishful thinking. We can directly influence the odds our children will sleep better throughout life. In spite of concerns some-times raised, sleep training itself has been shown to be both safe and effective for children's emotional development.[10] It requires only two parental disciplines: (1) establishing a set routine and (2) implement-ing the routine consistently.

Researchers reporting in the journal *Sleep* reviewed fifty-two stud-ies involving various sleep-time approaches on more than twenty-five hundred children from infancy to age five.[11] They found that virtually all pediatrician-sanctioned approaches should work, sometimes after a few days. The one consistent finding was . . . consistency! As long as parents stick with a plan, no matter how challenging, most children develop healthy sleep habits.

Here again, building consistent routines makes parenting easier. Any habit established in early childhood is likely to persist into ado-lescence and beyond. It is far easier to teach your toddler how to calm down and fall asleep than to convince a media-addled, sleep-deprived teen to turn it all off and get under the covers.

Reinforcing sleep habits (sleep training) as early as possible is a parenting benchmark and a cornerstone of adult self-care. When chil-dren push nighttime boundaries, parents become chronically overtired. That makes them less likely to maintain necessary routines in the first place, which sets up a vicious cycle. Our child cries and pleads and we're too tired to wait for him to stop. But "only tonight" does not mean much to a child. Joining us in bed or acting like a jack-in-the-box for two hours can take on a life of its own.

Kids aren't going to be the ones who decide when it's time to sleep alone. That type of thinking happens through a whole lot of mature, long-term EF-based planning. Why go to bed when it's more fun to stay up? Sleep training is a short-term, exhausting challenge for most families, but parents must decide when to start. Brace yourself for a few hard weeks, but keep your eyes on the prize. Parents and kids both feel better when sleeping through the night.

Establishing a bedtime routine largely comes down to new habits and consistency. Kids don't have the perspective to realize that sleeping through the night makes their lives—and their parents' lives—better. The short-term effort involved in sleep training leads to tremendous long-term gains. Here are some guidelines for starting your own sleep-training routine:

Decide when bedtime starts. We all fall asleep easiest when our internal clock (our circadian rhythm) coincides with when we're turning out the light. For a child put to bed too early, falling asleep is a challenge. Too late, though, and children pass their "sleep window" and become restless again. An appropriate bedtime aims for head on the pillow (not starting bedtime itself) as the body slows. A consistent bedtime in and of itself has been correlated with cognitive performance.[12]

Start an hour before "lights out." Determine when you think your child should be asleep and start bedtime around an hour earlier. If that timing is unclear, monitor it by observing when your child seems to slow down a little. Whatever you decide, set a reminder alarm if you tend to lose track of the time yourself.

Establish an environment of calm. Children need guidance on how to ratchet down from the day's activities. The idea of "sleep hygiene" means a habitual plan for settling, including activities such as showering or bathing, quiet games, and reading. In spite of a common misperception, screen time actually wakes the brain. The brain needs free time from electronics before falling asleep, so make this break part of the routine too. Avoid horsing around or other activities that rev up the body; exercise aids sleep but only when separated from bedtime itself. Offering a choice between reading and sleeping is one great way to encourage a lifetime habit: *Bedtime is 8:00 p.m., but you can read until 8:30 p.m.* It's one of the healthiest nighttime choices children can make.

Encourage sustainable "sleep associations." Children seek reassurance when falling asleep each night and several times during the night while cycling through light sleep. They unconsciously check for a comfort object or a parent. Avoid making yourself their sleep association; if they have learned to seek *you*, they often wake when you are not there. Instead, create a space where your child feels safe and comfortable, and encourage an association with a soft toy, picture, or whatever else soothes.

Ease yourself out. If you have become part of your child's falling asleep, gradually reduce your presence. To move a child out of your bed or to get yourself out of their bedroom, pick a start date. Anticipate several weeks of disruption whenever you change the rules. Fade out your physical presence, perhaps sitting near your child's bed, then moving toward the door gradually over several weeks. Or fade the time between checking in on your child, returning after five minutes, then stretch it to ten minutes a couple of nights later, adding on more from there.

Place a child who wakes up and gets out of bed back in his bed without discussion. Avoid letting bedtime become a source of attention. If your child needs something, provide it with minimal conversation. If he needs nothing except to avoid going to sleep, direct him dispassionately but firmly to lie down again. Anticipate your child's needs by making sure they pee, have water, or eat before bedtime if those are frequent requests after lights-out.

Monitor your child for anxiety. If fearfulness or anxiety undermines sleep, discuss ways for managing these challenging emotions with your pediatrician or another health-care professional.

Tie the bedtime routine to a reward program (optional).
Offer stickers or points toward a long-term goal for each
night that your child successfully follows your guidelines.

Consider This

Sharing a bed with your child is a controversial topic.
The American Academy of Pediatrics recommends
against it, as it has been linked with sudden infant
death syndrome (SIDS) and other physical risks to
infants.[13] A baby in bed also makes adult sleep difficult,
adding to exhaustion and cutting into physical
intimacy. Infants should remain near enough for
our attention when needing food or a change, but a
separate crib works best.

Modeling Media Use: Parents First

MILLIONS OF DOLLARS are spent to make sure we spend as much time as possible on our devices. Kids are uniquely susceptible, and games are designed to keep them from ever wanting to end playtime on their own. For most families, it's entirely up to parents to decide what's healthy.

Phones and computers are products, honed to hook us and hold our attention. They are, of course, not inherently bad. They *are* tools that require us to step back periodically and make sure we're making independent decisions, not blindly following behind people making money through our tech use. There's little incentive on their end to guarantee our long-term health and safety. That is our job alone.

Remember, living well with technology comes down to a strong brain manager. Most parents are aware that "too much" screen time is bad for kids. But we rationalize the time anyway, maybe finding it easier to assume it benign (or rationalizing our kids' phone use as okay in comparison to their friends' use) rather than fight over it. It feels easier to assume the norm is fine than to address media excess.

Parents feel overwhelmed, as if this is the inevitable state of our world. Complaints arise that kids are sucked into more and more television, video games, and computer time. In the end, though, any individual can make a different choice. Nothing is stopping you.

Technology even affects our relationships with our children. Background television left on without anyone watching on its own cuts down on the length of conversation and social interactions with them.[14] Phones have been shown to disrupt conversation too. Even when face down on the table, they draw our attention away from the immediate world around us.[15]

Children develop productive, safe relationships with technology—and have fun with it too—through what we demonstrate in our own relationships with screens, through what we teach our children in our discussions with them, and through clear limit setting. Many parents find that technology is a useful babysitter at times—dinner needs to be made, and that is reality. But the tendency toward expanding screen hours becomes hard to battle once it begins. Early habits have been linked to adult habits, unsurprisingly. Avoid the issue by setting clear rules from the start.

As with any part of life, we can aim for awareness and clarity in choosing how to live with modern technology; in other words, we can be mindful. Technology-based products grab our attention and hold on whether or not that's in our best interest. They can provide organization, efficiency, and entertainment but can also distract, disorganize, and disorient. Pause, check in with yourself, and resolve to keep technology in its place by making skillful use of it throughout your life.

Here are some ways to cultivate awareness and clarity around technology:

> **Check in on your tech use.** Perhaps the most fundamental starting point for changing a habit is recognizing it exists in the first place. To that end, various apps provide a daily summary of our phone use. On the computer, other programs do a similar job. Don't forget, open-ended downtime (sometimes called "boredom") is often where creativity arises. Consider regular breaks from whatever causes you stress, whether a few days away from headlines or avoiding social media (and all the inherent parenting chatter) for a time. A list of some of these resources to help monitor usage can be found at howchildrenthrive.com.

> **Support healthy habits.** There are more healthy-living apps than can be easily summarized. Your phone can monitor your daily activity and can offer new fitness programs. Nutrition-dense recipes, food diaries, and more are available. Or you can use your phone to monitor how much and what quality sleep you're getting.

Stay on task. How often are you on your phone while with your children? Or pulled from a task by an urge to check your phone? Hopefully, when we need to be engaged or productive, we resist checking news, messages, or playing games. If not, there are ways to keep ourselves on task using specific apps that lock out the distractions.

Be proactive about notifications. Shut off notifications and alarms that aren't vital; we don't need to know immediately about every email, social media posting, game update, or news event. There's no need to permit default settings on phones and computers to rattle our minds all day long. Check in with programs only when you have time for them. This also helps you attend to the reminders you actually need to see.

Practice gratitude. In the classic novel *White Noise* by Don DeLillo, a crisis lurks in the background, undermining everyone's well-being, a feeling similar to what many people experience in our media-driven world. Download an app that prompts you for a daily gratitude practice, which research shows increases happiness.[16]

Practice mindfulness. Any new habit requires consistent, sustained effort before becoming a routine, including getting started with mindfulness. Multiple apps provide guided mindfulness instruction, and most also include a prompt for daily practice. My meditations can be found at howchildrenthrive.com, but plenty of other resources are available.

Create mindful contact reminders. For common contacts who cause you stress, set their image to something peaceful or that makes you smile. Remind yourself, with a picture or words, to pause and settle before answering. Of course, pick something that if accidentally seen by someone else will not anger them or get you fired.

Consider This

In a world drowning in television and computers, make yourself a role model. Establish healthy habits early by keeping the television off during meals and turning it off when no one is directly watching. During family time, check in with your own habits and bring your attention back to your children whenever possible.

Managing Media Through the Ages

THE INVENTION OF the wheel changed humankind. Seemingly for the better. But here's the thing: It was a revolutionary tool, not a product. Of its own merit, it took over civilization. It didn't have a marketing department to guide it along the way.

Technology today—any kind of technology—is a tool and also a finely honed product. Marketing departments make certain that we want more and more of it. Our phones and computers are specifically manipulated to hook us. We rely on them and want to spend more time with them. They distract and grab our attention and entertain, often far more than we might otherwise choose for our lives.

As noted earlier in Putting Your Kids on a Media Diet, the place technology has in our culture is historically more like cigarettes (a real health risk) than rock and roll (a perceived risk). Generations ago, some of Billie Holiday's music was banned, yet of course there was no actual connection between her songs and bad outcomes for kids. It was also not that long ago that doctors promoted cigarettes. Just because something seems normal doesn't mean it's okay. Cigarette sales to minors were even legal in some states. Clearly, that situation turned out less than ideal.

Through lots of research and advocacy, we realized that tobacco needed to be reined in. Smoking is harmful. Technology is not inherently a problem in the same way; it's how we use it. Right now, it isn't totally fine to let things be only because it feels like the inevitable norm. It takes effort to push back and create boundaries with our children—but doing so has direct benefits for them too.

What our kids are exposed to today is very different than when we were young. The level and type of violence seen in cartoons, sexual content, and direct-sales pitches aimed at developing minds is nothing like it was a generation ago. Around the Internet, the ability to learn and find information online has huge potential value. But because every act of violence, pornography, and more is also now one click away, children rely on us for moderation more than ever.

Most children and teens will not come to a balanced relationship with screens without parental support. It disrupts their sleep, pulls from activities that might benefit them more (such as reading or outdoor time), and can facilitate social crises. Most kids, given the option of eating sugary cereal for breakfast, cake for lunch, and ice cream for dinner, would happily go down that path if allowed to by adults. While we wouldn't allow that behavior around food, we tend to trend that way around technology.

Treat screen limits the way you would deal with a child who wanted nothing more than to eat chocolate cake fourteen hours a day. Television and video games are mindless, which is why zoning out in front of a favorite show feels like exactly what we need sometimes. But for a growing mind, passive activities are not nutrition; they are nothing better or worse than dessert after a meal. Nothing is wrong with some cake every once in a while or some occasional screen time, but enough is enough.

Let's consider mindfulness again for a moment. Mindfulness means living life with more awareness and less reactive habit. For a parent, that means not aiming for perfection but continually taking the time to pause and readjust. We're all flawed and make mistakes, but we can keep trying to raise resilient children the best we're able. As they need our guidance around nutrition, exercise, sleep, and physical health, they also need it when carving out a healthy place for technology.

Push back against mindless screen habits. Wherever technology truly helps, or entertains as a balanced part of life, that's perfect. When its use is driven by boredom, fear, or compulsion, mindfulness means pausing and redirecting once again.

Nothing much has changed in terms of how children develop or the role parents play. The world may be busier and more technology driven, but kids develop as they ever did. Parenting in the digital age means the same thing it did in the Stone Age: Children require affection, firm limit setting, and a mindful, aware, clear-sighted approach that guides them toward a healthy lifestyle, from sticks and stones through smartphones and television time.

> ## Consider This

Aim to use technology with intention, instead of inertia. Check in with your family's habits periodically. Make sure there is a healthy *who, what, when, where,* and *why* component when establishing guidelines around your kids' screen time: Who is on a screen? What are they watching? When are they watching it? Where in the house are they? Why are they on a screen?

Part 4

MINDFULNESS AND FAMILIES

✱

Mindfulness in parenting matters. It's not a specific thing to do; it's a way of life. Mindfulness is a long-term opportunity to build traits that lead to greater happiness and the capacity to manage challenges. It is about real-life situations and building skills rather than a simple buzzword. In fact, there is no more direct way to train attention and executive function than with mindfulness. For the advice and practices that follow, start with yourself, share with your children if they seem willing, but remain confident that your own mindfulness practice will educate them. Read this section straight through, and then sustain a daily mindfulness practice based on what you discover. From there, remember that mindfulness for kids almost always starts with parents.

The Antidote for Perfectionism

MINDFULNESS IS sometimes portrayed as a setup for personal failure (*Parenting is hard enough without aiming to be mindful all the time*). Mindfulness often conjures images of relaxation, stillness, or acting in some idealistic, staid way. There's an assumption it means always being calm, serene, and in control. That perspective misses the point of the practice. Mindfulness is not a drive for perfection. In fact, it's quite the opposite.

Being mindful starts, in part, with accepting the fact that we cannot ever be fully mindful. Our brains aren't wired that way. And life itself is unendingly uncertain and unpredictable—being a parent tends to bring that idea into clear focus. Imperfection is the norm. It's how we live with these facts that influences our moment-to-moment well-being.

So sure, one aspect of mindfulness is aiming to be *more* focused with our attention. That's because, otherwise, most of us spend a lot of our time doing one thing and thinking about another. While that's going on, we're not aware in any useful way about what we're doing, saying, or thinking. Not only do we miss out, but we fail to notice the assumptions and choices we're making throughout the day, inside our family and out.

Even when practicing mindfulness, however, we cannot pay attention long. Over and over, we get distracted within our own minds. When we notice ourselves lost in our thoughts, once again we bring ourselves back . . . until the next time. The practice has distinct benefits—otherwise, it would be silly to bother—but there's no particular endpoint. In fact, rather than getting caught up in being solemn and serious about mindfulness, it's fairly useful to bring along a sense of humor. Our minds often do what they want without us, an odd state in which we live. We're spending a lot of effort aiming for something not fully attainable. We're trying to be more attentive and less reactive and less driven by habit—and then become caught up in it all over again.

Mindfulness, however, also does not mean *I'm perfect exactly the way I am*. It's not that "Life's all good." Clichés like that don't mean much. We all could use some improvement, and sometimes life isn't particularly good. Instead, when we recognize that we're lost, feeling once again that we "should" be a perfect parent, we practice letting that thought go and then return to doing our best without extra layers of self-judgment.

Surfing the never-ending waves in real life, we aim to improve while not judging ourselves for needing to. We must readjust and try again both in mindfulness practice and in the rest of life. After all, what can any of us do except pay attention to making skillful choices, work diligently at what it seems we can influence, and try to be at ease with all the rest?

Mindfulness is meant to capture a way of living. Another way to view it looks something like this: We have a whole lot easier time managing life when we are aware of what we're doing instead of getting by on autopilot. Without effort and attention, our lives follow the same old mental ruts day after day. One of the first things apparent when we pay more attention is that our mind has a mind of its own. It creates ideas constantly—some useful, some random, and many habitual. On autopilot, we keep on living this way, whether or not it's to our benefit or our family's. We accept how we do things, and our thoughts, as fixed and factual. But, as the saying goes, there's no point believing everything we think.

One common mental pattern is called "the inner critic." Like the two old guys in *The Muppet Show* balcony who provide unrelenting heckling, the inner critic insults and judges, mostly without reason: *You're not good enough. You should have done x or y but definitely not z again*. It's not about self-improvement, making amends, or fixing what needs fixing—we want to build those traits. The inner critic represents mindless self-judgment that undermines well-being and affects our interactions with everyone, especially our kids.

When we take that critical voice at face value, it fuels the desire for perfectionism: *I blew it, I should be better at _____* (fill in your own habitual voice). Even if there is some reality to address—maybe we would benefit if we were a little less reactive or hit the gym more—the incessant negativity isn't helpful. We can aim for change without constantly deriding ourselves along the way.

Many of us spend a lot of energy trying to convince ourselves this judgmental voice is wrong by pushing ourselves endlessly or ruminating about our perceived flaws. We fear the criticism reflects something truly wrong. But the inner critic does not evenhandedly grade our performance in any useful, valid way—it's just an old habit. Pondering our own worth, skills, or prospects can't much influence this inherently irrational voice, since it's not reality-based to start.

When we recognize the inner critic as nothing more than an entrenched mental habit, we shift our relationship with it. Instead of trying to pacify the voice of judgment, we name it and create some distance. (*Thanks anyway. That's judgment, and now I'm coming back—not wrestling with you today.*) Instead of believing the nagging, perfectionistic voice, we pause, glance toward the balcony, and come back to real life once again.

Stuff happens, not all of it great. We mess up, and so do the people around us. As Jon Kabat-Zinn suggested in his classic first book on mindfulness practice, *Wherever You Go, There You Are,* ease means finding comfort in the midst of "the full catastrophe" of life. Our family is what it is, often chaotic and perfect in its imperfection.

A formal mindfulness practice is an acknowledgment that if we aim to build certain traits, we access them more readily in daily life. If you want to be more aware, responsive, emotionally balanced, compassionate, or anything else, it takes effort. It doesn't require being perfect. When you hear that voice taking over, it's an opportunity to notice the thought and practice putting it aside for a while.

We all benefit when we take a few moments to focus our attention (without expecting stillness). Or settle our busy minds (without expecting stress to go away completely). Or build awareness of the assumptions and habits that drive us (without blaming ourselves for those tendencies in the first place). Or develop more compassion in our lives (even though some people absolutely, totally annoy us).

There is no perfect. If you're judging yourself while practicing mindfulness, notice the habit. If you have a false perception that you can ever be perfect, you'll end up even more stressed. Be aware of that idealistic picture, and then let it go. You're flawed and so is everyone else in your family, but when you aim for improvement, everyone benefits. Mindfulness isn't perfectionism—it's the antidote for perfectionism instead.

> ## Consider This

Notice if you're getting caught up in following all the advice in this book "perfectly" or comparing your own parenting style to an impossible ideal. Notice the anxiety and fear it may provoke, and then set it aside. Take a moment to acknowledge everything you're doing well and the steps and plans you've already taken and made.

> ## PRACTICE   Working with Your Inner Critic

Practice noticing your inner critic during everyday life. Each time you notice the critic, pause and try this simple practice:

1. Breathing in, recognize the voice of criticism and whatever it's implying about you. Acknowledge that experience without needing to either banish it or rationalize it: *This is how I feel right now.*

2. Breathing out, let go. Focus only on the sensation of breathing as best as you're able, without striving or forcing anything. Instead of wrestling with self-judgment, see it for what it is, and turn your attention somewhere more useful. Wish yourself well, like you would a close friend in distress. Picture freedom, relief, or ease with each outbreath, as an intention for now or sometime in the future.

3. Repeat as necessary.

Attention, the Negativity Bias, and Stress

TRY THIS EXERCISE for one minute: Pay attention to nothing. Not an idea, feeling, thought, sound, or fear. Just pay attention to absolutely, completely nothing. That, of course, can never happen. Your mind went somewhere, whether it was a beach fantasy or thinking this exercise seems bizarre. Our minds pay attention all the time, and not exactly where we choose.

Where does our thinking mind go? For stretches of time, exactly where we want it—engaged in an activity, problem-solving, or enjoying our lives. Sometimes it seems to go three places at once, torn between helping with homework, looking forward to bed, and resolving a problem at work. Sometimes it's caught up in the past (*Everything would be different now if only . . .*) or future (*How will he ever hold a job if he can't do his homework with me?*). Sometimes it's distracted, like that feeling of playing catch at the playground for half an hour before we notice we've been back at the office the whole time. We aim to bring our full attention and our best intentions to parenting, and then our mind takes itself anywhere other than where we want it to be.

Our minds play tricks on us in these distracted moments, falling into countless habits that make our lives more difficult. One of the strongest tricks is called the negativity bias. We preferentially attend to and remember whatever seems off, unpleasant, or dangerous. While it serves on one level to keep us safe, this skewed perspective swamps our well-being when we lose touch with all that has gone well. Recognizing this tendency, we can actively train ourselves to notice—and appreciate—everything else going on in life.

Awareness of how attention works can change everything. We can begin to explore where our mind goes when unattended. When we habitually pay attention, we change some fundamentally disruptive habits, making decision-making and problem-solving easier in our homes. If we don't see our patterns for what they are, they'll drive our life forever. When we start recognizing how the mind behaves, we guide our attention where we choose more often. Consider these five key patterns to start building awareness of how we pay attention:

Happiness and attention. A Harvard study showed, separate from whether something was inherently enjoyable (like sex) or not (like a chore), that one of the next best predictors of happiness is paying attention to whatever it is you are doing.[1] Of course, our children know this too. How often do we hear, "Dad, why aren't you paying attention to me?" Taking care to give attention to our families when we are together can be its own practice: *I'm here . . . now I'm daydreaming . . . now I'm back to painting with them again.*

Autopilot and attention. We tend to go through life doing one thing while our mind is elsewhere. Without real attention, we act out of reflex, missing assumptions and choices we've made. We're reacting, bouncing between grabbing for whatever might bring short-term happiness, and recoiling from irritants and fear. To exert free will, we practice awareness, noticing what's happening, for better or worse, pausing long enough to respond, and then choosing a path forward: *Whenever I'm tense, I push my kids to work harder . . . I'd like us to forget chores today instead and go see a movie.*

Multitasking and attention. The brain cannot multitask. Literally. When we try to multitask, we're actually ping-ponging between ideas and tasks. Although multitasking seems useful, it has been shown to increase errors and decrease efficiency. For mindless tasks, such as folding laundry, multitasking may have value (although research suggests that giving full attention to even mundane tasks may decrease stress). For all the rest, attending to each activity, one after the other, decreases stress and increases performance, even though the world pressures us to do everything at once instead.

Negativity bias and attention. What keeps you up at night—the nineteen things that went well or the one that didn't? The tendency to dwell over past regrets and future fears skews our perspective, making us unhappier and, of course, more stressed. We are wired to focus on the negative, so it takes effort to steer ourselves otherwise, not through candy-coating life but recognizing whatever goes right day to day and moment to moment. We all have stuff to fix and things that go wrong, but plenty goes well most days too.

Stress and attention. Unpleasant things come up far more than most of us would wish, from little irritations (*It's too warm in here*) to all the major catastrophes of life. Sometimes it's not so much that we overreact but that our attention holds onto a stress-making thought and won't let go. Maybe we then add reactive thoughts about how life "should" be and ratchet up our discomfort. Ideas like *This will never end . . . this always happens to me . . . I/he/we/they should know better* grab our attention and make uncomfortable moments far more painful than they would otherwise be. Focus attention for a few breaths somewhere less charged, and the stress cycle often abates.

Our happiness relies on how we choose to pay attention, instead of remaining on mental autopilot. We can't be happy living in the past. When we get caught up in regrets, we're undermining how things feel now. We can't be happy in the future. We can plan for change, but if happiness is always *When I finally go on vacation again . . .* or *When school starts going better, . . .* that gets in the way of our experience today. For our sake and for our children's, increased attention and awareness increases our well-being and changes how we live.

When it comes to paying attention, there's the old joke about a man stopping someone in New York City for directions and asking, "Pardon me, how can I get to Carnegie Hall?" The answer, of course, is, "Practice, practice, practice." Our attention will never stay totally focused exactly where we want it, an important trait to recognize. With practice, however, we more habitually let go of rumination and distraction, instead of staying stuck in our ruts. It's possible to shift our attention more often toward what we choose, noticing our successes and our children's and all there is to appreciate about our lives far more often than being guided by our idle minds that naturally want to gravitate toward worry, negativity, and stress.

Through paying attention, we live more freely. We care for our family's problems more flexibly, stand up for ourselves more easily, and become kinder to ourselves and everyone around us. There's no perfect, only more awareness and continual steps toward a less stressful life.

All of that starts with nothing more than paying attention.

Consider This

Focused attention from caring adults is the starting point of most behavioral programs for children, even actively defiant teens. Make a practice of giving full attention to your kids for at least a few minutes every day. Try the same with easy activities for yourself, noticing when you find yourself drawn elsewhere. Redirect your attention back to the present, and notice the physical sensations, thoughts, and emotions that make up this enjoyable and positive moment in your life.

Feeding the Right Wolf

A BOY SAYS to his grandfather, "How is it you never seem to get upset? Don't you ever feel angry?"

His grandfather replies, "Of course I feel angry. I sometimes think there are two wolves inside me, each of whom fights to tell me what to do. Whenever something angers me, one of the wolves is full of fire and wants to attack and act nasty. The other is calmer and makes better choices. But they're both always there."

And the boy asks, "But if they always fight, how do you know which wolf will win?"

The grandfather answers, "The wolf that wins is the one I choose to feed."

Human nature hasn't changed much since this Native American folklore tale was created long ago. We all have impulses and habits, some healthier than others—our inner wolves. What has changed is that, in this modern technology era, we are uniquely barraged with information and imagery, much of it disturbing and upsetting, that feeds a particularly angry wolf. One wolf stands for our most resilient, strong, skillful parenting side, the other all the fear and anxiety and perfectionism that undermines our best intentions.

Our brains are hardwired to notice potential hazards, a vital bias when in actual danger. The problem is, even when we're not under acute threat, upsetting things grab our attention more than positive things. Our mind craves relaxation and happiness (or maybe simply a good night's sleep), yet lighter moments of life pass often without much attention or recognition at all.

The news media seemingly thrives on this all-too-human tendency. Graphic headlines and shocking stories fill our daily experience and raise a specter of danger around our children. The news appears intent not only on informing but on riveting our attention in place, presumably to increase ratings and revenue. However, this isn't entirely the media's fault, since we're the ones choosing to watch. Who hasn't compulsively stared at repetitive, grueling coverage of a tragedy?

So what can be done? For starters, we can decide to feed our healthier wolves more often, the part of our self that is grounded and at peace. That can relate to being more selective in our approach to the Internet and modern media. There's an expansive middle ground to explore between "well informed" and "force-feeding an angry wolf until it consumes everything around it." Healthy choices for our families require some balance between staying educated and keeping above the fray.

Another way of finding this less-charged space is through mindfulness, which loosens the grip of negativity for a few minutes, through actively focusing our attention elsewhere. In everyday life, that could also mean recognizing that doing altruistic things may improve our own state of mind.[2] Some people sustain a daily gratitude or compassion practice as a reminder to focus on positive experiences in their lives and in the world around them. For our ongoing inner wrestling matches, these moments build an advantage for the clear-sighted wolves inside.

A core message within mindfulness practice is the challenging reminder that, throughout the world, everyone is driven by similar desires. Each person may picture it differently, but we all want relief from our suffering and to find happiness for ourselves and our families. Those with whom we most disagree seek their own image of relief, however twisted it may appear. In any situation, we can fully defend ourselves and still understand this basic reality: It doesn't require condoning someone's behavior to realize that they're suffering. In some situations, taking steps to eliminate someone else's pain may even protect ourselves down the line.

Scary as our daily lives seem, these facts hold true. Amazingly, apart from a small minority, nearly all the billions of people on this planet exist peacefully together while trying to navigate their lives. Many people are intentionally helpful to each other. If not that, at least they leave each other alone. On any given day, almost everyone on this planet, thankfully, behaves well despite headlines that may make us feel rotten about the world.

This is not meant to be naive. There is plenty to address emphatically around anyone who put others in danger, and plenty to change about how we collectively live, much of which directly impacts the future of our children. For all that we'd like to see change, most people remain remarkably skillful at managing anger and frustration and following the rules, right down to the Miracle of Rush Hour, when thousands of drivers hit their breaks in sync, stop at red lights, and stay on the correct side of a swath of yellow paint on the road while we safely get our children from point A to point B.

As Grandfather suggests in the folktale, remain aware and feed the wolf of your choosing. Emphasize what is going well without sugarcoating the rest. Take firm action when you can while also making choices about where to give attention in life—and in your mind. If enough parents focus on the healthier wolves more of the time, maybe we can even influence the tone and content of tomorrow's headlines and the world our children inherit from us too.

Consider This

Try out a nightly gratitude practice for several weeks, either in a journal or using a phone app. Without forcing yourself to feel anything, pay attention to something positive. Write down at least one thing for yourself that went well or to appreciate. Consider making a similar practice at the start of mealtime or bedtime with your kids.

Eating as a Metaphor for Mindfulness

NEWSPAPER IN HAND, spoon in mouth. Nothing illustrates the need for practicing mindfulness more than our habits around food and eating. Exploring how we relate to food is a wonderful chance for parents and children to develop mindfulness in an unforced, you-got-to-eat kind of way.

Getting out of autopilot around food and eating—noticing our food choices and recognizing that far more than hunger drives our decisions—allows us to cultivate mindfulness both with eating and throughout life. Because in the end, where else in life are we so often utterly mindless? We eat the way we eat because that's what we do. We plow through our favorite foods by the handful so quickly that we don't even taste them. We slow down and suffer over each spoonful of what we dislike. We know exactly what style of eating would be healthiest but never manage to make it happen.

And then, for many of us, one day our religion calls for a fast. Or maybe the doctor does: "No eating until after your lab test tomorrow." And what happens? For 364 days of that past year, we acted the same when hungry. We got edgy and irritable, or we grabbed the nearest candy bar. Then, out of the blue, for this one day, our perspective changes all at once. Just like that, without that much stress, our habits drop away. It's uncomfortable. We're hungry. We get irritable, but probably less so because we know we cannot eat. We push aside all our eating habits because we have no choice: *I'm hungry, but I'm going to have to wait.* It's challenging but doable—proof that it is really, really hard to change eating habits—but not impossible.

That, of course, is mindfulness in a nutshell. Aware of annoyance or stress, we accept what's unpleasant. We choose to refrain when we feel that's the best course of action. Then, when it's time to end the fast, we eat, and for the first time in ages, we notice, enjoy, and savor every bite as if it matters.

Everyday eating can be entirely caught up in habit. Instead of focusing on broad changes all at once, consider how your family eats, and select one pattern you wish to change. Label that one small pattern "habit," and then set an intention for something different. It might be personal: *Instead of fries, I'll order salads*. It could be for the family instead: *I think I'll stop keeping chips around the house*. Start small, and expand change gradually from there.

You always have the option of paying attention. Encourage a family practice of putting down your utensil between bites and consciously deciding when to take another one. Pause before making food choices—not to give anyone a hard time, but to be aware that you have a choice. When cooking, pay full attention to the process, allowing your mind to focus on the activity instead of being caught up in worries, plans, or other thoughts—and consider bringing your child into the preparation too.

> ### Consider This

Mindful eating can happen with any food or meal, at any time. Just pay attention in an unforced way as you might to a unique and spectacular meal, without even needing to slow down all that much unless that's what you choose. Use this experience to build your capacity for giving life the full attention it deserves.

► PRACTICE   Eating Mindfully

For a more formal practice of awareness while eating, try this (a guided version is available at howchildrenthrive.com):

1. Select any food, ideally something you can hold in your hand. Imagine you have no idea if it's edible. Take your time exploring each sensation that follows, along with whatever thoughts and emotions you notice about your experience.

2. Begin with vision: What colors are present? What does light do when it hits the surface or when you move the object around? What else do you see?

3. What does the food feel like? Does it have any weight? What changes as you move it in your hand?

4. Does it have a smell?

5. Does it make a noise when you move it around?

6. Pause for a moment and notice: Where have your thoughts gone? Are you feeling anything emotionally? Are you bored, restless, or feeling awkward? Are you excited about trying this food, or doubt it will be tasteful for you? Recognize those experiences, and then return your attention to the exercise.

7. Choose the moment when you'd like to place the object between your teeth, then pause before proceeding.

8. Now put the object in your mouth, adding the sense of taste. Observe taste, as well as what changes with each of your other senses.

9. Chew just once, then pause. Check in with your five senses again. Check in with your thoughts and feelings. When your attention strays, return to the practice again.

10. Continue chewing with the same intention. Does the taste, smell, or physical sensation change?

11. Before swallowing, pause and decide when it's time to do so, practicing intention. Then swallow. Can you feel the food moving all the way down to your stomach?

12. Apply this approach with each bite, and continue until you decide the practice is done.

Managing Stress from
Our Toes to Our Head

A 2016 STUDY suggested that people who have better body awareness tend to feel less stressed.[3] That's no surprise, perhaps, if you've already been practicing mindfulness, but it may seem odd otherwise. Stress causes a physiological response, such as an increased heart rate or sweating. People in the study who reported themselves less overwhelmed by a challenge noticed their physical state sooner than others, and brain scans showed they better reined in anxiety before it escalated.

This relatively simple idea illustrates a somewhat complex concept around stress management and mindfulness. Through a mindfulness practice called a "body scan," we typically observe physical sensations from our toes gradually moving up to our heads. But what's the benefit of knowing what's going on with our toes?

Mindfulness is meant to be practical, and once again, this study shows why. The body scan monitors subtle physical shifts constantly occurring in our bodies. Observing in this way is not an abstraction but rather a path to a less stressful life. Over time, we develop the type of awareness that experts in the study discovered for themselves—a useful perspective for the average frazzled parent. When unaware of our physical experience, we may miss the first signs of stress.

Left unattended, stress amplifies itself all day long. A thought or experience sets us off, and that affects our bodies and our moods. How our body feels and our emotional states affect how we think. Thoughts lead to more thoughts, and on and on. Awareness of that pattern, and actively choosing to step out of the cycle, makes a world of difference. From the moment we wake and wrestle the kids out the door to the bills and the calls and the news headlines and everything else, stress leads to more stress if we don't take care. Since it's far easier to settle ourselves when mildly stressed than after fight or flight takes over, body awareness helps.

Of course, it's not specifically about stress, it's about using awareness to live differently. Our bodies reflect our emotions and provide early warnings of our mood shifts. Even more subtly, our bodies influence how we feel. For example, one study showed that poor posture (the slouch used while staring at a phone, for example) can make our moods worse.[4] Being aware of what's up in our bodies is one vital way of managing our lives.

Practicing mindfulness isn't specifically meant to be about our own well-being. More globally than that, it affects how we live with others, including our families. When we develop the capacity to notice physical experience, instead of following down the typical path of avoidance, we practice pausing and perhaps redirecting ourselves out of our mental ruts. Catching the cycle early, we settle our racing hearts and minds before anxiety takes over and drives how we act. At any time during the day, we can use our body to settle our mind in this way.

> ## Consider This

Begin to notice how your body physically feels under stress, especially your early warning signs. Those could be tension in your face or back, queasiness in your belly, holding your hands in a fist, or practically anything else you find. Practice taking a breather as soon as you feel the signs of stress in the body instead of waiting until you are swept away once again.

> ## PRACTICE   Body Scan Meditation

Download and try a body scan for yourself for a period of time once daily; one is available at howchildrenthrive.com. During this practice, pay attention to your feet first (for example, the feeling of their touch on the floor), and then move your attention, body part by body part, all the way up to your head, letting go of any effort to make anything specific happen along the way—you can't force yourself to feel relaxed. Also notice areas of tension and stress that you can let go of, even a little, as you move your attention. The body scan is a great introduction to mindfulness for kids; try adding it to their bedtime routine.

Emotional Rescue: Using Mindfulness to Reset Your Internal Life

THE IDEA OF EMOTIONAL AWARENESS can seem almost mundane. On some level, most of us recognize its benefits. Yet being skillful with emotions isn't only about recognizing when we feel happy, angry, or sad. Awareness means noticing *all* emotions, whatever arises, and then making an active choice about whether it's best to act or choose to leave things alone. Whether for parents or children, an ability to recognize, talk about, and manage emotions allows for a much more even-keeled life.

As with body sensations, mindfulness of emotions builds an awareness that profoundly impacts our lives. It's barely a cliché that bottling up emotions creates internal pressure, like shaking a bottle of carbonated soda. And it's not a platitude that describing how we feel decreases the hold emotions have over us. But those ideas only scratch the surface. Without greater awareness, unattended emotions steer us away from long-term happiness and well-being.

All emotions have their reason to exist, a point made resoundingly well in the computer-animated, coming-of-age movie *Inside Out*. There's no point suppressing or being annoyed by any of them. Joy feels great, but anger, sadness, fear, and disgust all play a role and provide an opportunity to peek inside our minds. A negative emotion signals that something needs addressing, such as *I'm sad because I'm grieving and need my friends* or *I'm fearful because this project is a challenge and I need more time on it*. Recognizing emotions in this way in and of itself can guide us in taking care of ourselves.

But not every mood shows up because of life experience. We have fleeting ups and downs driven by our own inner chemistry and yet often blame something or someone outside ourselves for these haphazard states. We easily misattribute a downturn to our child, partner, or an external experience—someone or something must be responsible for our feeling bad. Needing comfort, we may accidentally rattle the people who might provide it: *I haven't asked and I've been prickly like a cactus to him, but still, if he really cared, he'd come sit with me.* In our minds, someone becomes part of the problem who really isn't, and then our behavior changes how they act, setting off a chain reaction, ultimately pushing them away and confirming our fears.

Sometimes a mood is nothing more than a mood, whatever its cause. At times there's nothing useful to be done except notice it and, for a stretch, let life be. Instead, we often seek solace in reactive habits, lashing out or shutting down, or whatever else offers temporary relief. Yet those mindless habits of suppressing and reacting can make things worse and fail to fix the underlying cause. Some moods show up and leave of their own accord, awful or wonderful or anywhere in between, and the healthiest response may be leaving them entirely alone.

When we fail to acknowledge emotions, we magnify unpleasantness by skewing our perceptions of the world. When angry, we're more likely to see others as angry. When sad or anxious or whatever else, those states affect how we interpret our experience. Our emotions change how we think, and those thoughts undermine our emotions again. It's that same cycle again, as thoughts and emotions affect how we physically feel, which then influences our emotional state. It all continues unabated if we don't take effort to steer ourselves somewhere healthier. This pattern is one of many ways that stress, unattended, perpetuates itself.

Negative feelings hold on tight and then trigger reactions that pull us further into mental rabbit holes and exacerbate challenging states of mind: *Oh no, here I go again; I'm not capable of taking care of myself . . . I hate when I get like this.* What was going to be a short downturn becomes a crisis, a mental cyclone triggered by fear, remorse, and self-doubt. That storm swamps us, and we end up avoiding activities, people, and even ways of thinking that would otherwise help us feel better.

When we build mindful awareness, we notice our emotions more clearly and with less resistance. We recognize our mental habits and actively leave things alone for a moment instead: *I'm in a bad mood, it's not my fault or anyone else's, and it will pass.* Whatever our urge—to ignore emotion or to react to it—we can work on something new. If something useful and healthy can relieve an intense emotion, go for it. The rest of the time, observe, seek comfort when you can, and then define the next skillful step forward for yourself.

Consider This

Pay attention to family messages about emotions. Do you accept and discuss emotions with your children, or tend toward denying or ignoring? Even saying *It's all okay* can be a type of dismissal—*It's clearly not okay—can't you see I'm hysterical here?* Supply both comfort and empathy: *I know that hurts. Come here, you're going be all right.* The same can apply to discipline: *I see you're angry, and you still cannot talk to me like that.*

PRACTICE Paying Attention to Emotions

One practice with emotions is summarized by the acronym RAIN:[5]

R = Recognize your emotions. A more nuanced ability to describe emotions all on their own may change your experience.[6] When you see nothing more than anger, that's all there is. When you nuance that experience into fearful resolve about an uncertain future, you feel different and may become better able to seek useful solutions moving forward.

A = Accept your emotions. You cannot force yourself to feel any specific emotion; they come and go all on their own. Fighting with or refusing to acknowledge a bad mood often makes it worse. Notice what's there, and for a few moments accept it as it is.

I = Investigate your emotions. Turn with curiosity toward your emotional experience. Does it wax and wane? Does it cause a physical sensation in your body? Alter how you think and perceive the world? Is there a more accurate word to describe your emotion than you'd typically use?

N = Nonidentification. You are not your emotions. Your knee hurts, not you, but so often we say, I *am* sad. You are you, and you happen to feel sad. Allow the emotion to run its course. This will be easier to do when you remain less caught up in it.

Awareness of Thought:
Finding the Light in Mental Storms

OUR MINDS MAKE THOUGHTS all day long, some useful, some random, and some exhaustingly habitual. But realizing that some thoughts are just thoughts and some habits just habits creates space from rumination, worry, self-judgment, and other patterns that undermine our well-being. We don't have to believe everything we think.

Caught up in mental breezes, gusts, and storms, most of us take passing thoughts at face value. Something drifts by and we grab hold: *I wonder why no one makes savory ice cream flavors and I need to call a tutor about my child's reading and that new phone looks so cool!* Some thoughts are valuable, amusing, or useful while others remain reflexive, random, or even troublesome. Not all of them reflect anything valid or useful.

An ability to work with our own patterns of thought is quite practical, as has been shown by clinicians studying mindfulness-based cognitive behavioral therapy (MBCT), which integrates traditional therapy and mindfulness.[7] One premise behind MBCT is that specific ways of thinking magnify life challenges. A practice of mindful awareness allows a new approach to these difficult mental patterns.

One of the best-studied MBCT programs regards treatment of depression. Before MBCT, someone with a history of depressive episodes might notice an emotional shift and get sucked into a vortex of despair: *I'm sad today. It's happening again, and I have that interview Friday; this is more than I can handle.* Within that cycle, the downturn escalates and entrenches itself. Participants in MBCT are encouraged to reframe how they approach their moods. Encountering strong negative emotions, mindfulness guides us toward noticing and reframing triggering thoughts: *I'm not feeling great today, and I'm afraid it may get worse, but right now I'm coping.* That concept applies as much when encountering a mood as with worry that a child may fail school or get a job or anything else thrown in our parenting path over time. There's an experience, and then there's everything that follows.

Whether we want them to or not, ideas come and go like clouds in the sky. A disturbing image of the future isn't the future. A past event is forever behind us unless something needs to be done about it now. It isn't easy to let go of sticky thoughts, but it's useful to recognize how seldom they're tied to reality.

Thoughts are nothing more than mental concepts, not actual facts, and many add stress to already stressful situations. There's a time for problem-solving and analysis, for creativity and random fun. There's also a time for letting things alone, as not all ruminations, assumptions, memories, or imagined futures are worth, quite literally, a moment's thought. Thinking can be the problem, not the solution, when there's nothing to fix or to be done.

For example, consider self-judgment again. Our inner heckler imposes a far harsher perspective than our closest family and friends would ever take toward us. It hurts, and maybe makes us feel incapable of change, and yet most of the time the inner critic isn't judging us on anything particularly valid: *You'll never change . . . you shouldn't dwell on things so much . . . you should know better.* It's a learned mental pattern, nothing more or less.

Caught in the mental squall, there's not much point yelling or trying to force the critical voice away. Instead, we can sometimes realize we don't love the fact that our inner weather has turned nasty, but not contest it either: *That's the critic spouting off again, thanks anyway.* We don't have to validate the criticism by engaging with it quite so much.

Other mental routines further skew our perspective. Try this: Reflect on a past decision that went well and one that wasn't your finest. Then picture an ideal future for your child and one that worries you. Now, focus on what makes you most proud about yourself and then what you least like. For each reflection, which mental response holds your attention longer?

For most of us, whatever seems off or dangerous stands out. If ten things go perfectly one day but you feel you screwed up one interaction, which one sticks around that evening? Making skillful choices, repairing a mistake, or planning for the future is quite different from becoming swamped by hypothetical or long-past events.

On a smaller level, perhaps it plays out like this: Our daughter has the thought, *I don't want broccoli tonight*, but instead grumbles aloud, "I hate broccoli." From there we have our own thoughts: *You loved it yesterday. Why always so difficult about food? You need to eat more veggies or you'll never be healthy*, but instead we reply, "You've always liked broccoli. Cut it out." She pushes back and stands up for herself, "I do hate it. Leave me alone." She shoves the plate away. Which leads to more thoughts and reactions, ours and hers.

The escalation takes on a life of its own. Now maybe her one idle thought moves toward an actual aversion when, really, there was nothing more than a thought to start, something that rattled you and rattled her but wasn't all that serious. Noted without all the debate, reactivity, and circular patterns it triggered, it might have passed on its own.

Sometimes a habitual discussion entrenches itself too, long past whatever first set it off. Broccoli isn't a big deal, but debates about food (or school, exercise, or whatever else) live on. *I say this, she says that*, and off we go—unless one of us chooses not to take the bait. There's value to remaining aware, noting patterns, and sometimes letting things be for a bit to see what happens next.

Whatever we discover, we don't have to identify quite so closely with much of what our mind creates: *That's a disturbing story about the future I've fashioned, but I'm doing what I can. I'm rehashing that decision again—enough already, I did the best I could.* Such understanding creates a huge shift even during the hardest times: *I'm in a dreadful mood, but it's distorting my perspective and it will pass.* Stepping back, we more easily give ourselves, and our children, room to move forward again. Without retreating, wrestling, or fighting with it all quite so much, we become far more discerning in how we live.

Mental habits can be both useful and far from useful; to sort them out, we first must acknowledge their influence. Without judging ourselves as flawed for whatever we find, we can set new intentions. That might apply to anything, from how we talk to our family and friends to managing stress and even to how we vote in elections. Guiding ourselves out of reactive stress mode, we observe and move toward clarity.

Not that it's so easy to let go of what drives us, or even to figure out which thoughts require action and which do not. It's not our fault that something feels unpleasant or we get stuck in an old mental rut. We may easily blame ourselves for having less-than-useful habits in the first place. But we're all constantly experiencing all kinds of thoughts and can do no better than the continued effort to work on what we're able. There's never a need for perfect.

Consider This

Mindfulness doesn't mean staring at your life through a microscope—it's not meant to increase thinking about thinking. Instead, you create mental space that leads to more awareness of what influences your life. If you're thinking about *that* concept too much, that's another thought too. Notice that, and maybe it's time to get into the woods, knit, or whatever else helps clear your head.

PRACTICE   Watching the Weather

A mindfulness practice called "watching the weather" allows us to sit and observe thoughts as they come and go like we might do lying back in the grass on a warm spring day and watching the sky. We create space between thoughts and the reflexive beliefs and actions we bind to them. The aim isn't to disconnect from reality; at some other time, problem-solve or run with a creative idea. But for now, take a few minutes to give yourself a rest and observe the passing mental clouds.

So much of what feels fixed or permanent turns out to be assumption, conjecture, or fantasy. Note the directions your mind takes. Label what you observe—thoughts, feelings, and habits. Note them all as best as you can, and practice letting them alone during a few moments' break.

Along the way, it can be useful to question what you observe: Is it true? *I'm not good enough to handle this. If she doesn't get her act together, she'll never get into college.* But is it true?

Shoring Up Resilience Through Mindfulness: It's All in Your Mind

IMAGINE TWO EQUALLY TALENTED graduates at their first jobs. Within a year, downsizing gets them both laid off. One becomes caught up in thinking he's failed: *I was never good enough. My boss hated me.* The other decides, *I wanted this job so badly. I better fix my resume and learn how to deal with a difficult boss better.* Who moves through adversity more quickly?

The same attitude carries over for parents around daily routines, school, or anything else. If one parent expects bedtime to be stressful and another feels it should happen without much adult effort, who has a harder time sticking to sleep training when it gets challenging? Our perspective toward whatever we encounter in life fundamentally changes how we experience it.

Stress itself can be defined as the *perception* that something is more than we can handle. When we frame challenges as surmountable, we surmount them more easily. When we frame them as opportunities for failure, we more often fail. That may sound like the most hackneyed, clichéd advice ever, but it is a foundation of resilience research.

Resilience relies on how we perceive our lives. So maybe we get queasy watching our child on stage for the first time; anxious and concerned, we start ruminating. Within those thoughts exist layers of assumptions, perspectives, and mental filters—*I didn't prepare her enough; she's going to embarrass herself; I must do something to save her.* If we feel our role is to protect kids from *everything*, that moment on stage becomes miserable. If we recognize we cannot shield our children from every hurt, but we've done our best, the experience changes—*I'm almost as stressed as she is! Hope it goes well, but I'm here if it doesn't.*

Perception itself is malleable. In fact, this idea is a focus of the military's resilience training for soldiers.[8] Participants explore mental traps—habitual distortions that undermine emotional well-being. These pitfalls might represent thoughts like *Asking for help is an admission of failure*. They include catastrophizing the worst possible outcome of every situation or, alternatively, minimizing and ignoring whatever overwhelms. An overly active inner critic may continually let us know we are not good enough to manage. All these distortions represent filters that twist perspective and pull us away from resiliency.

With mindfulness practice, we learn to hold these patterns to the light and question ourselves: What is valid, if anything, and what isn't useful? Is our view inflexible, reactive, or full of doubt? Without belittling ourselves or forcing ourselves to be unnaturally positive, we observe with curiosity and redirect ourselves until new habits develop: *She's on her own up on stage now; I'm nervous but need to let go.*

Uncertainty and change are inevitable in life—doubly so for parents. Instinct drives us to worry and protect endlessly because we care more than anything about our families. But if the only relief we seek is striving to battle uncertainty into submission, that causes needless stress, as certainty never happens—and too much stress undermines not only how we feel but the choices we make day to day.

Laboring under the misperception that parenting worry is ever going away only makes us feel worse. We cannot and should not aim to control everything. Rather, we can shift our perspective to accept that stressful things happen over and over again. When we try to fix everything we face and reach for a perfect picture of happiness, we undermine our best intentions. The perception that parenting or any other part of life can be anything other than imperfect and changing pushes us far from our most skillful and resilient selves.

You can begin to separate your perspective from the experience itself. Many attitudes toward adversity seem like factual statements: *Those people are like that. My child will never . . . I'm not the sort of person who ever . . .* Notice those habitual thoughts, and ask of each, *Is it true?* Drop your assumptions and predictions for a while, and see what changes.

Try catching yourself with this simple STOP practice: *Stop* whatever you're doing; *take* a few slow breaths; *observe* what's going on around you and in your mind; and *pick* how to proceed.

The following suggestions, adapted from recommendations of the American Psychological Association, provide a framework for shifting perceptions and building resilience:

Make connections and accept help. Value relationships with close family members and friends, prioritizing time with them, and reach out for support when needed.

Monitor for mental traps. Whenever undermining habits appear, pause, label them (*catastrophizing again*), and redirect. For example, if you feel shut down by fear, acknowledge that fact, then refocus on something useful to be done as a first step: *If nothing else, I'm calling the pediatrician today and getting a referral.*

Nurture a positive view of yourself. Catch your inner critic in action, set it aside, and focus on your own strengths instead: *Thanks anyway, I wish I'd done it differently but I didn't. What would be the best thing to do now?*

Aim to accept that change and uncertainty are a part of living. One common misperception that undermines well-being and resilience is fighting with whatever is truly beyond our control. Even when something upsetting happens, separate that experience from a broader expectation that it "shouldn't" have happened in the first place.

Develop step-by-step goals and take decisive action. Rather than detaching and wishing stress away, stay proactive. When tasks seem unachievable, ask, *What's one small thing I can accomplish that moves me in the direction I want to go?*

Take care of yourself. Engage in activities that you enjoy and find relaxing. Taking care of yourself helps to keep your mind and body primed for resilience.

Consider This

Children learn more from what you *do* than what you *say*, so your resilience—the way they watch you approach adversity—affects theirs. Pay attention to how you experience challenges. Note how your body feels, your emotions, and where your thoughts go. Are you projecting your fears about the future? Are you caught up in regret or resentment? We often add to unpleasant moments in ways that make them even more difficult.

Unhooked from Reactivity,
Hooked onto Wisdom

WE ALL KNOW what it feels like to get hooked by something in life. It happens every day. Little things and big things—a look, a thought, an experience—grab us viscerally. A tear in our jacket, a tone of voice, a failing grade, an unexpected rainstorm. The hook is a burning, restless urge that craves relief because we feel attacked, disappointed, uncertain, or confused.

Getting hooked, we easily lose track of our best intentions. A meticulous sleep plan collapses as a visceral sensation takes hold, and we leap into reaction. We finally go downstairs to spend a moment with our spouse and then hear a child tiptoe down the stairwell, for the third night in a row. Without reflection, we yell, "Get up those stairs! I told you no more of this!" Or instead, we're having a calm morning, but it's time for the bus. We ask our daughter to get her backpack, and she responds in that exact tone, "Why don't *you* get it?" It digs to the root of our brain, it seems, and then . . . *Let the battle commence!*

Parenting can seem like one long experience of feeling hooked. Your worry and uncertainty are real. Without them you'd be numb. You're a parent: *Oh no, he wasn't invited to the party.* It feels miserable for you and for him and then you're on the phone nagging that other parent in a way you know you'll regret in an hour. Unmanaged, the hook pulls you to your verge—off balance and tugged by an aching desire for relief.

When we get hooked, what happens next? Most often, an immediate, impulsive reaction. Then regretting that choice, quite often we're hooked all over again—*I can't believe I did that*—and then we buy an excessive gift or overexplain or break into the cookie jar.

An entirely new way of living starts when we practice dropping the hook, acknowledging when we feel off, and then aiming as best as we're able to let things be: *He's got to eat better, but there's nothing to be done about it tonight*. We may even notice in someone else, *Wow, he's totally hooked. No point in saying anything more now; let's come back to this later*. It's not a call to ignore anything about our lives or force ourselves to feel okay. It's quite the opposite—an opportunity to realize that sometimes we're feeling jittery and lacking a better option, but we're okay with that uncomfortable fact.

Often it feels as if the hook and its reaction are the same thing: When I'm hungry I get irritable and must eat right *now* (even if that means grabbing whatever crap is nearby instead of waiting a few minutes). When I'm scared about the future, I ruminate until I come up with a solid plan (even if I already have one and am running myself in circles). Yet that visceral feeling of being hooked and what we do about it are more nuanced—there is a sensation and then an urge for relief. And then there is that urge and what we choose to do with it.

This type of intentional pause doesn't mean becoming passive. It's creating a space to act wisely. For example, say you're embroiled in yet another argument over bedtime and, exhausted yourself, feel the urge to capitulate: *Fine, go read in my bed (again)*. Dropping the hook, settling, you may find the space to pause and stick to the plan: *I hate the fact that we're still wrestling over bedtime, and I want my own rest, but you've got to go back to your own room*. Noticing yourself hooked lets you act decisively as often as electing not to act at all.

Working with the hook is immensely challenging and does not mean we're suddenly okay with suffering. Getting hooked is inevitable; what we do about it is not. Without awareness, we snap at a child, so they snap back, and we end up in a ritualized sparring match. We feel a desperate need to escape, so we shut down. We fall back on more troublesome habits, like drinking or fighting. These habitual reactions quite often grant, at best, a moment of respite while whatever triggers us remains. We find temporary relief but complicate our lives instead of finding any true resolution.

Sometimes there is nothing more useful than allowing a situation to run its course without adding anything: *I'm hooked, and what makes most sense is to be patient with my distress while I get on with my day instead of having that same conversation once again.* Instead of reflexively trying to fix how we feel, when we recognize that we've been hooked, we can practice pausing. Relax as best as we can. Refrain, even if for a moment, from falling back on habitual reactions. And then start over when we get caught up in it again.

Parenting will often lead us to feel unsettled, since so much is out of our control. For example, if a child has a learning disability, you may be getting him tutoring, and he's in a good school, and at the same time, there's no way of knowing for sure what's going to happen. So you feel somewhat concerned indefinitely, which is natural. If you continually give in to the urge for certainty, you may continually fall back on overplanning, ruminating, or numbing yourself in some avoidant way, none of which brings anything productive to your family life.

If you have an actual itch, it's usually okay to scratch, and when there's something useful to be done for your children or yourself, go for it. With other itches—like being annoyed that bedtime has gotten off track or uncertain what to say next during a disagreement—your best option may be to acknowledge the hook and then firmly pause. Make a joke, let it slide, or flat out acknowledge aloud exactly what's going on: "I'm taking a breather, because I'm seriously rattled." Settle yourself and even for a brief moment, let go.

There's some discomfort in life that cannot be touched. It's just there. It makes utter sense that we feel triggered by anxiety around our children or plenty of other aspects of life that don't feel comfortable. In any situation, whatever we do (or choose not to do) *next* could make it better, but could also drive the hook deeper. Acknowledging our discomfort, we may find it best to live with how we feel until a better option becomes clear.

Since it's natural to get hooked, we should not blame ourselves or expect to move beyond ever feeling rattled. There's a problem, there's getting hooked by the problem, and there's how we react next. There's fear, the visceral response to fear, and how we respond to fear. There's the uncertainty of parenting, and how it twists inside us, and most practically there is what we do when uncertain.

> Consider This

We can choose to work on letting go of the habitual ways we react when hooked because, in the end, being reactive is kind of a silly way for the mind to behave. We know better, and cannot always help ourselves anyway. Sometimes we can find peace, and often more happiness, noticing the inevitable discomfort while letting it be. Learning to pause when we get hooked may break the reaction and get us—and our child—off the hook.

> PRACTICE   Getting Unhooked

When you notice the hook and an urge to react, try this 4 Rs practice.[9] Whatever sets you off, choose not to grab onto the hook. Recognize what you feel, and let things be for a moment.

1. **Recognize** the feeling of being hooked.
2. **Refrain**, for a moment, from doing whatever you typically do. Pause, take a few breaths, and let things alone before taking a next step.
3. **Relax**, letting go as best as you're able of any sense of constriction or tension. If you see something useful to be done—go for it. If not, practice letting things be instead of falling back on reactive, less productive habits.
4. **Resolve** to keep working on it. Old habits change slowly, not all at once.

See a Habit to Break a Habit

STUFF HAPPENS, not all of it great. We want to guarantee our own well-being, and our child's, but we cannot. Stress itself has been honed down to a one-line description: getting what we don't want or not getting what we do want. We'd tell anyone else to expect the unexpected and then get caught off guard anyway.

You're at a restaurant with your preschooler and a waitress puts down a milkshake on a nearby tray. As you turn to look at the menu, your lovely preschooler grabs the glass, falls out of his seat, and gracefully lands in the lap of the stern-looking woman in the next booth—with the milkshake in slow motion tumbling onto them both. In that moment, hooked and on edge, what's the first, gut-level reaction that comes to mind? One person might reflexively lash out at their child. Another person might blame the waitress. Another might want to hide under the table. For someone else, that first feeling might be self-criticism—*I should have known better.*

We all have habitual paths that we've developed in life. Many have value, or once did, or do in one situation but not another. The way we address our sales team may not go over at a family picnic. We settle into routines that keep the day moving and take care of our children. We have some routines that are perfectly useful and save energy, but often they become mindless and rote.

Limit setting is a perfect example of how these mental tendencies influence families. We fall back on old habits when off-balance or distracted. As we grasp for perfection and recoil from imperfection, our habits drive us to be too strict or too lenient, particularly when exhausted or stressed. For our best friend, we'd recite a step-by-step rationale for why limits matter, then at home we become lost in the chaos of everyday life.

The capacity to choose exists only in the moment between something that triggers us and what we decide on next. Simply paying attention, without judgment or expecting perfection, creates new options. Without judging ourselves for having them, we can explore our own tendencies and therefore create an opportunity for change. Common patterns that undermine behavioral planning or almost any other part of life include:

> **Grasping.** We exhaust ourselves with efforts to make everything fit our visions and preprogrammed expectations. We often hold onto stories about how things "should" be (*I'll be happy when life is exactly as I pictured*), or a desperate desire to control, plan, and fix everything. You might avoid rewards or setting limits due to a belief that they *shouldn't* be needed because your child *should* know better. Or you might grasp onto that transient moment of happiness when your child gets a gift or a treat, and you fall into a trap of indulgence; it's a limited, false belief that getting stuff makes anyone happy for long. Gifts are great and surprises even better, but they don't relate much to long-term well-being.

> **Aversion.** It's natural to avoid what we don't like and push away anything unpleasant, so maybe we collapse when facing an angry, upset child. Perhaps we have a picture of ideal parenting in which children rarely cry, arising either from our own sense of compassion or because a parenting book suggested it was possible. So when our kid melts down because he wants that toy in aisle three, we give in. Maybe we struggle enforcing limits and avoid seeking help out of worry that we'll be judged for not doing it on our own. Accepting things as they are, even when they're unpleasant, allows for consistency, flexible problem-solving, and more resilience.

Feeling overwhelmed or burned-out. Sometimes being a parent, or life in general, may feel like too much to manage. We may have a metaphorical—or literal—urge to go back to bed and pull the covers over our head. A mental fog prevents us from handling a situation. At times like these, it may feel easier to let our kid do whatever he wants: going to bed late, making questionable food choices, having poor manners, or skipping chores. When we are exhausted, it's far easier to let things slide, despite our best intentions.

Restlessness. Sometimes we feel impatient and want to force changes to happen right away. When anger, anxiety, or uncertainty take over, they may cause us to leap into compulsive action rather than sticking with a well-considered strategy. For example, we might impulsively toss out our entire behavioral plan, though we know with patience that it may work out fine as it is. Or we might create yet another plan out of worry that we need to be doing something more active to guarantee success instead of patiently sticking to what we've decided is best.

Self-doubt. And then there is parenting doubt, in drips or deluges, arising and receding like the tides: *I should know better; I don't have the strength to change this; if only I were more like my sister*; and on and on. Once again, by noticing and labeling our inner heckler, we more easily let go.

Begin to notice your personal style around parenting. When difficult moments arise, pay attention to thoughts, emotions, and physical sensations. Then notice tendencies toward grasping, aversion, feeling overwhelmed, restlessness, or self-doubt. When you catch yourself, name what you see, and steer yourself elsewhere if needed. In each instance where something isn't working well, investigate with compassion and awareness. Maybe new limits are called for as your child grows up. Maybe you made a choice that hasn't worked out and you need to adjust. Or maybe, when you pause to reflect, you'll see that despite your fears, everything is fine as is.

> Consider This

Habits are hard to change. Pause often and redirect yourself with patience. And when you manage a situation as you intended, pay attention to that too, and give yourself full credit for the accomplishment.

> PRACTICE   Fifteen Breaths

Here is another in-the-moment mindfulness break, similar to the STOP practice (see page 188): When you feel yourself distracted, rattled, or feeling hooked, pause. Count fifteen breaths, focusing on the physical sensation of breathing. Breathing in one . . . breathing out one. It usually takes around a minute or less. If you lose count, restart wherever you last remember. Gather your attention, and then choose what to do next.

Self-Compassion and the Average Parent

REFLECT FOR A MOMENT on a challenging situation where you felt you screwed up. Maybe you missed an important deadline and now your child can't go on the school trip. Or you really wish you had had him evaluated for learning disabilities three years sooner than when you got around to it. Bring to mind anything that doesn't feel like it was your finest moment. What thoughts and feelings come up? For most people, there's a tendency to be harsh. A litany of criticism takes over.

But what would you say to your best friend? Most people would reassure: "Everything is going to be fine. It's not that big a deal. You're such a great parent; everyone makes mistakes." We would be fully empathetic for a friend, and yet we are almost abusive about ourselves.

When we are overly guided by such inner voices of criticism, it undermines our happiness. It leads to stress and burnout, and it affects how we treat others. Conversely, when we develop more self-compassion—a strange concept for many of us—not only do we feel better, but motivation improves. In spite of any learned belief that perfectionism and self-judgment drive us toward success, they actually undermine our well-being and performance.

Dan Siegel, MD, the renowned psychiatrist and teacher of mindfulness, has researched the concept of building "coherent stories" about our childhoods. However challenging, inappropriate, wonderful, consistent, or inconsistent life was, we make sense of our past. Resenting our siblings unfairly when we're fifty because they had more freedom than us affects our lives today. If we're able to step back and recognize that maybe that past experience kind of stunk but now we're different with our own kids, a whole new possibility arises. According to Dr. Siegel's research, when we stop struggling with our past demons, our children feel more secure.

Making sense of our past is a complicated emotional process. There probably is plenty we wished never happened, some of it potentially quite awful. A coherent story never means condoning inappropriate behavior or forcing ourselves to feel okay about a loss. It also doesn't trivialize seeking therapy or blaming anyone for their own childhood trauma. Whatever our life experience, we benefit when reframing our inner narrative to focus on strengths, personal connections, and opportunities for future growth.

Far too often, though, we burden ourselves with blame or judgment: *I should have known better. Everything would be different now, if only I . . .* Our stories get mixed up with family narratives, all the rationalizations and interpretations that may put us in a box, place blame, deny, or even ignore harsh realities.

Mindfulness at its simplest means nonjudgmental awareness. That includes an honest appraisal of our own life experience. A coherent view almost always includes a mix of both positive and negative experiences, and then ties those, in a comfortable way, to our adult selves. We became who we are now because of our past, for better and for worse. Without that step, that attempt to seek clarity, our children may become burdened by our past demons.

We can build a capacity to notice regrets, anger, and confusion, to recognize when we get caught up in visions from decades ago, and then practice letting go: *Right now, this is who I am.* Those ongoing childhood resentments, lingering all the way through family Thanksgivings today, affect us—and our children. Sometimes we may realize that something was painful and disappointing long ago without needing to rationalize why it happened, and create more space for change.

The past has passed. The future *will* unfold, which we influence only in this moment, through what we do or plan or choose to do or not do. An ongoing struggle with either may pull us far away from what's more immediately best for our families right now. Whatever is going on today is going on today.

We can spend our lives wrestling with resentment, blaming ourselves for whatever we've done or failed to do. That constant comparing and belittling undermines our well-being and changes how we interact with people. But what would we say to a best friend in the same situation? "It wasn't your fault. You're doing great; keep working at it." With practice, we find the space to treat ourselves like we would our closest friends.

Kristin Neff, PhD, is probably the foremost researcher around the benefits of this self-compassionate view. Her research shows that, counter to what many people fear, with self-compassion, motivation tends to increase and the ability to move toward unique goals grows. We give ourselves leeway to take manageable steps, to stumble and recover, and to be less than perfect along the way. An overall sense of well-being becomes more consistent as self-compassion develops.

Self-compassion replies to the heckler inside. That voice rails at us that we're not getting "it" right, although there is no specific "it" to parenting nor a perfect way of doing "it." It's a voice of comparison, perfectionism, and holding ourselves up to a false ideal blown out of proportion by a Facebook page. We compare ourselves to everyone around us, to standards of success, like money and grades, social status, or our own perfectionist pictures. Whatever we find, nothing changes that voice much, and it rages on.

> ## Consider This

Think for a moment how you'd advise a friend to handle their own self-judgment, someone who says, "I'm so down on myself" or "I never get anything right." You'd probably make a joke, or you'd reassure. You'd tell them, "Mistakes happen. Come on, we can do this together." You'd rally and motivate and do everything possible to dismantle arguments created by the irrational, illogical voice of judgment. What would you say to that younger you, struggling to overcome adversity? You deserve the same benefit of the doubt, from not only your friends, but from yourself.

How can you build self-compassion? When you're feeling down on yourself, try this exercise.

PRACTICE Self-Compassion

1. **Breathing in, note to yourself that this is a *moment* of suffering.** Accept that you're feeling off, without blame or judgment. Accept that you feel you've made a mistake or have a regret. Recognize, and perhaps say to yourself, *This is part of life for everyone.*

2. **Breathing out, focus on how you'd approach your loved ones in the same situation.** Wish yourself well. Bring to mind, if you like, what you would say to a close friend—or what your closest relative might say to you. Focus on a wish for relief, forgiveness, or freedom, as you would for someone else.

Common-Sense Compassion

COMPASSION IS DEFINED as a feeling of deep sympathy and sorrow for another who is stricken by misfortune, accompanied by a desire to alleviate the suffering.

While compassion means acknowledging fully someone else's suffering, it doesn't require condoning their behavior. It doesn't even require relieving someone of their pain if there's nothing to be done. It's a recognition, as the band Poi Dog Pondering sings, that "everybody's trying to figure it out." We all struggle and do our best by definition. Who tries to screw up their own life?

You'd think having compassion for our family would be the easiest thing in the world. Of course, it's not that simple. We don't see eye to eye with our spouse about a situation and our resentment grows. Our children annoy us and we lose touch with their perspective entirely. Caught up in the moment, we want our own security and relief, sometimes shutting down our larger perspective on life.

An ex-Marine once told me that basic training was his first exposure to people from all over, and he learned right away that everyone everywhere just wanted to be safe, fed, and have a job. Stopping to pay attention to life as it is, we realize we're all driven by similar desires. But life is uncertain, and without awareness we react and push back and make things worse. Even a misguided behavior is driven by what someone thinks will find them (or their family, friends, or community) safety and happiness. That's the reality for me, you, and everyone else too.

With our families, even discipline can start with compassion: "I understand you're angry and hurt, but talk to me like that and you're in time-out." A brutal tantrum in the store is driven by pain, a desperate need for that toy. We can remain open-hearted and supportive while wrestling with the most difficult situations.

Building this compassionate perspective leads to research-backed changes. Self-compassion, giving ourselves the same benefit of the doubt we would a close friend, has been shown to improve resilience, motivation, and relationships.[10] Studies also show that acting compassionately increases our own happiness and resilience; take time to help out someone else, and we end up feeling better. From preschool programs through adulthood, mindfulness programs increase empathy and giving, along with neurological growth in related areas of the brain related to compassion.[11]

With our families and friends and in the larger community, practicing compassion means taking a moment to reflect on our universal suffering and desire for relief. It isn't naive or passive. Our own flaws and problems must be addressed with clarity and purpose. There are individuals who act inappropriately, and many societal ills require fixing. Yet everyone everywhere is struggling in some way, from our own homes all the way to a random stranger in a grocery store across the world. It's not hocus-pocus to recognize that much of what's scary about the world arises from people suffering.

For the well-being of your own family, guiding children toward compassion makes their world safer. Lashing out verbally (or worse) might feel like we're protecting ourselves or our children, but we're not. Fear, conflict, and stirring up anger all lead to more fear, conflict, and anger. Protect yourself if truly in danger, while also realizing that when we attack someone else quite often the threat returns ten times over. Only through breaking that cycle, diffusing tension and pain, does the world become an easier place. Alleviate someone's suffering, and in a very concrete way, the future in which your child grows up changes for the better.

> ## Consider This

Compassion for others usually starts with taking care of ourselves. When we feel more settled and resilient, we interact with the world more openly. When we're caught up in self-abuse, self-criticism, or just ourselves in general, that undermines how we treat others. To consistently offer our best wishes for anyone else, our work starts with us.

> PRACTICE   Compassion (Lovingkindness) Meditation

Try a compassion practice yourself. You can download a guided version online at howchildrenthrive.com. Beginning with ourselves, we offer wishes that we find safety, health, and ease, and then we extend that compassion outward to a friend, a stranger, and onward. It's meant to be unforced, not tying ourselves into knots trying to feel anything specific, not absolving anyone of anything, and not putting anyone ahead of ourselves but not putting ourselves below anyone either. Take the time to wish each person safety, health, and ease, intentionally building a more compassionate perspective in everyday life.

Everyday Mindfulness

THE PRACTICE OF MINDFULNESS isn't an endpoint for its own sake; it's meant to affect how we live. It's showing children through our actions what we value. It's resolving to do what we can to take care of ourselves so we can care for our children. *Living* mindfully means making sure that our words and actions align with our beliefs.

We can, therefore, bring mindfulness to any part of our day—setting an intention, perhaps, to bring full attention to family meals, doing the dishes, or going for a run; and treating others with intention too, noting how we carry ourselves and speak, as well as the assumptions we're making about our children and the world. Living with mindfulness, we teach our children mindfulness.

Everyone at home contributes to the household atmosphere, but we directly control only our own part. When our mood is edgy and off, the household feels more edgy and off. How we speak to the family, manage stress, and set our priorities influences everyone. Our mood impacts our family and changes how they act toward us—and then toward each other.

Our behavior and choices create a ripple effect for our children all through the day. If we yell nastily as our child races to get on the bus, how is he going to treat other kids when he sits down? If we're warm and supportive, how might that change his social behavior? Our choices create an unavoidable domino effect far outside our families.

No matter the situation, all we affect directly is how we choose to act, or not act, throwing fuel on or dousing fires. In a moment where our child is completely off the rails, we redirect, stand firm, and seek resolution, all with continued awareness that our own actions change his. The basic rules of cause and effect apply across all aspects of life.

Of course, we'll never be perfectly serene all the time. But what, then, is our attitude when our personal weather turns foul? Even *those* times, grumpy and irritable, create an opportunity to demonstrate mindfulness, realistically accepting our mood, its effect on the family, and cleaning up after the storm by making amends, setting new intentions, and reconnecting.

A classic saying advises, "Before speaking, make certain your words will be an improvement on the silence." What you say and do, how you carry yourself, and even your emotional state make a tense conversation more likely to escalate or deescalate. There's nothing more we can do, though, than listen, adapt, and manage our own side. If we have a reactive, snippy child, does that more likely persist if we meet it with reactivity and snippiness, or another path? Here are some steps to take in working with mindfulness and difficult situations within your family:

> **Pause and move out of autopilot.** Step-by-step, skillful action pulls together all of mindfulness practice. Pay attention more fully, seeing things exactly as they are: *I've prejudged her this time around; let me listen first.* Pause, catch yourself, and check in: *I'm hooked, angry, and about to say something I'll regret. She's totally caught up in it, not thinking clearly, and neither of us can communicate well right now.*

> **Notice whatever impacts your experience.** With any challenge, the situation is likely far more nuanced than it seems. There's the conflict—an angry child flipping out in front of us. There's the physical sense of tension and stress taking over our body. There's our emotional state, whatever mood we're in plus whatever the conflict sets off. And there are thoughts, some of which may be quite unproductive—guessing what he is going to say, collapsing into fearful rumination (*Here we go again*), or leaping in a future of endless conflict.

Check in with your habitual reactions under stress. We can remain aware, again, of our habitual reactions under stress. Recognize all the entrenched, circular, not-so-useful patterns that exist within our families: *There it is, the bickering over homework . . . That's what I say when I'm stressed about money . . . This is what happens when she doesn't want to go to piano lessons.* Seeing them as habits, we can catch ourselves and choose to say something different or nothing at all.

Choose how and when to act (or not act). Bring awareness to your choices. Even when another person seems off base or out of control (especially then), the actions you choose will influence what comes next. That doesn't mean passivity; perhaps your typical habit is backing down too quickly. Consider the tension in the room and whether asking to pause and continue the conversation some other time makes the most sense. Realign with your best intentions while also standing strong.

Like all of mindfulness, skillful communication doesn't require micro-management or driving yourself crazy aiming for any unrealistic ideal. Instead of getting caught up in distraction, habit, and reactivity, remain aware of yourself before, during, and after any conversation. When it doesn't go well anyway, pause and try again. That's all.

Mindful living can be summarized as this: If you're *doing* something unskillfully, stop. If you're *about* to do something that seems unskillful, stop. If you've *just done* something you found unskillful . . . also stop, and go back and make amends.

> ## Consider This

If this discussion of mindful awareness makes you feel hyper-focused on your life, loosen up your practice. A classic metaphor is that compassion and paying attention (seeing the world clearly as it is) are two wings on a bird, each required in equal measure. We aim for endlessly empathetic parenting paired with a realistic sense of our own strengths and limitations, our children's strengths and weaknesses, and our evolving role in guiding them. See the world clearly, build compassion, and let go of the constant need to do, fix, or otherwise aim for perfect. Let go of the extra, and find more space to hang out, have fun, and enjoy your time together.

Mindful Kids in Context

MINDFUL EATING, mindful burgers, mindful sex . . . pretty much everything is mindful lately. Paying attention has value, but what's the goal of all that mindfulness?

Defining mindfulness exactly is like trying to define psychology or exercise in one line; you can do it, but it never quite captures everything. To summarize, mindfulness means aiming to be more aware of our immediate experience, with less reactive habit. Even that language may feel abstract to the average parent or child trying to find some peace and happiness. More than any single definition, what matters most is that there's an *intention*. We spend an awful lot of our lives reacting to things we like or dislike in ways that aren't always useful. When we break patterns and handle the uncertainty of life more easily, that's beneficial. However you define it, mindfulness means living with less mind*less* habit and more ability to manage the fact that life is awfully hard sometimes.

So what does mindfulness with kids mean? Another way of framing mindfulness is as a group of mental traits. It's not that anything specifically gets fixed by a practice of mindfulness; it's guiding children toward long-term skills that make life easier. We teach children to become more attentive, less reactive, more compassionate, and resilient. From that perspective, mindfulness is a way to build life-management abilities, but far from the only one. We offer children tools to handle the challenging road ahead through any means that fit.

When we say that mindfulness means "paying attention to what we're doing," we transfer this to our children by paying more attention to them when we're together. "Staying calm under pressure" means taking a few breaths and not blowing a gasket when homework falls apart. When we say to treat others with compassion, that starts with how we speak to the frazzled guy at the airport dealing with our flight cancellation. Acknowledging honestly and openly that no one is perfect, we also recognize that we won't stick to our own intentions all the time. We make mistakes and learn from them and keep going. Drawing our children into that part of life teaches them something too.

When it comes to *teaching* mindfulness, focus on the skills you want your children to develop. That matters more than whether they commit to a "mindfulness practice." We build resilience by developing EF and attention, emotional awareness, self-confidence, self-compassion, positive relationships, and all the rest that comes from being raised in a mindful, aware household. That doesn't mean specifically meditating, but it does mean emphasizing a balanced lifestyle.

Mindfulness implies living with clarity in a certain way. We guide kids to pay attention every way we can—by taking moments to pause and look at a sea shell or by prioritizing activities that build attention (like reading, chess, and board games) over those that disrupt attention (excessive screen time). We discuss emotions and describe our own emotions. We live compassionately, read books that reflect other people's perspectives, and generally immerse kids in compassion, while gradually considering if they're ready for a compassion-based mindfulness practice.

Mindfulness is a tool kit for a different way of living, one that provides kids skills to manage life on their own one day. The good news is, kids don't even have to practice it themselves to get there. They learn from watching us and from the overall way they live themselves. Of course, they eventually can learn from their own practice of mindfulness too. As you practice yourself, you'll know exactly how to encourage your children to join you (links to books supporting mindfulness in kids can be found at howchildrenthrive.com). But it's the big picture of how they are raised that counts most.

> **Consider This**

Imagine yourself from your child's point of view. How would your child describe you to a friend? What's fun and easy about you, what are your strengths, and what areas might you want to change?

Closing Thoughts:
Seeing the World as It Is

PART OF FEELING more settled as a parent is seeing the reality of child development clearly. That means guiding our children in the development of executive function skills that support long-term resilience. We can't build the road that our children will travel in life, but we can provide them the skills to navigate the path they end up following.

It's not that unpleasant things won't keep happening, but we change how we relate to them. When we spend our lives constantly wrestling with the stuff we don't have any chance of changing, and constantly striving to reach moments of perfection with the expectation that they are going to stick around forever, we end up more stressed and less happy.

Instead, we practice seeing our experience more clearly and accepting whatever is right in front of us with curiosity and openness. If something is not what we want, we feel compassion for ourselves, problem-solve, and maintain some equanimity when able. If we find what we want right in front of us for a stretch of time, we appreciate it without desperately holding onto something that's inevitably going to change. Our children grow into teens, and then eventually adults, and then leave our homes.

Everyone in life, despite how it seems from the outside, is trying to find some degree of happiness and well-being. Nothing is more uncertain and changing than being a parent. Seeing our children, ourselves, strangers, and the rest of the world through this clear-sighted, realistic view, aiming to change what we can and accept what we can't, and continually trying to sort through the difference, we can find a more settled, successful relationship with the awesome and rewarding, exhausting role of parent.

All we want is to know that our children are going to be fine, happy, and well adjusted, but in the end, there is absolutely no way to guarantee that. Things go well and we grasp onto them, hope they will never pass, aim to control our lives, and avoid inevitable change. Something becomes uncomfortable, and we hope it goes away, which is normal, but then we become too involved with forcing it away, reacting in ways that aren't always so useful.

So much of parenting is driven by hope and worry in this way. We fear whatever we cannot know and cannot control. That anxiety drives us to seek certainty even when there isn't any to be found—*I just want my son to be happy.* Grasping for control, wanting to be sure we have everything completely covered, we end up overscheduling, being too demanding or not demanding enough, or whatever habits consume us. Yet being comfortable with the discomfort of parenting is where freedom begins.

Being a fearless parent does not, paradoxically, mean being unafraid. Of course we feel fear. We're afraid we'll die young or our kids will. We're afraid our kids will be unhappy or unpopular or unsuccessful. We're afraid of the choices we make and don't make. It would be almost crazy not to have those types of fears. It's what we choose to do with them that matters.

Fearlessness means accepting those uncertainties and not being driven by them: *I'm nervous as hell about school. My son did poorly last year, but we've made changes and it's time to let things be.* There's an incredible vulnerability to being okay with being uncertain, sitting with the sensation of defenseless, objective acceptance. When you arrive, though, parenting anxiety slides away and a whole new level of comfort, ease, and fun begins.

Raising mature, confident, skillful children who treat others and themselves with respect often requires less, not more. Don't worry about consumerism, parenting trends, and all the things that obscure your own wisdom or cause you to ruminate about yet one more thing you have to do. Raising kids is infinitely complicated, and yet simple. Since you can't do everything, do your best. And since you can't protect them from everything, pass on the skills they most need to manage their futures on their own.

Let go, let go, let go.

Let go of perfectionism. There is no perfect parent. Children need a stable warm home environment. They need clear, dispassionate limit setting. What they don't need from you is any expectation of perfect.

Let go of consumerism. There's nothing more you need to buy or schedule. Prioritize what your children enjoy. Prioritize activities and, when needed, interventions they require. Otherwise, let go of any marketing-driven pressure to schedule or purchase more than makes sense.

Let go of the academic push. Children are children. We can't force them to develop any more rapidly than they naturally do. While we can encourage development at times, and while we need to catch up children who fall behind, in the end children require patience, direct instruction, and an education that emphasizes their overall well-being, including exercise, play, and family time.

Let go of fear. We're all worried about our children's future. We all need to plan and take care of what we can. Notice where fear and anxiety of not buying that one item or class that would set your child up for success takes hold, and let go. We can build our child's ability to manage their own lives, nothing more or less than that.

You know what's best for your children, whether around health and nutrition, or screen time, discipline, or anything else. When life gets in the way of your best intentions, redirect yourself back to your most skillful self, right up until you get distracted, and start all over again. You are by definition doing everything you should and can. Why wouldn't you? As often as needed, without judging yourself for being less than perfect, pause. Check in with life as it is. Come back to the unpredictable, aware, entertaining, perfectly imperfect family you intend to raise, as best as you are able . . . and watch your children thrive.

Acknowledgments

THERE ARE MORE PEOPLE to thank and acknowledge than ever, as I'm blessed with such an extensive and caring network of friends, family, and colleagues. So for starters, my family again, for everything I've been taught and their endless tolerance and support—my wife and children and parents especially. To all the friends who have been part of my family for so many years, your presence means more than I can say. Endless gratitude to Melissa Valentine, Leslie Brown, and Jody Berman, my insightful editors, and everyone else who has been so wonderful at Sounds True. Once again, thanks to Debbie Yost and Carol Mann for putting me (and keeping me) on this writing path, and Jennifer Swanson for research support, as well as James Marcotullio for some last-minute aid. Multiple friends and teachers have guided me professionally, including Amy Saltzman and Chris Willard, around mindfulness and family. Several people read drafts and provided feedback along the way, including Drs. Cynthia Braun, Dzung Vo, Jill Green, and Jorge Pedraza. Thank you to everyone at Mindful.org, *Psychology Today*, and *The Huffington Post* for early support of my work on this topic. Thanks to all the attending physicians and other professionals and staff at UCLA, Oakland Children's Hospital, and the Kennedy Center at Albert Einstein College of Medicine. And more thanks and gratitude for all the teachers within the world of mindfulness (some of whom I've never even met), including (but not exclusively) Sylvia Boorstein, Pema Chödrön, Mark Coleman, Jon Kabat-Zinn, Susan Kaiser Greenland, Derek Kolleeny, Jack Kornfield, Noah Levine, Sharon Salzberg, and Dan Siegel. Wishing you all, and your families, well!

Notes

Part 1. Brain Management as a Developmental Path

1. Walter Mischel, Ebbe B. Ebbesen, and Antonette Raskoff Zeiss, "Cognitive and Attentional Mechanisms in Delay of Gratification," *Journal of Personality and Social Psychology* 21, no. 2 (1972): 204–18.

2. Yuichi Shoda, Walter Mischel, and Philip K. Peake, "Predicting Adolescent Cognitive and Self-Regulatory Competencies from Preschool Delay of Gratification: Identifying Diagnostic Conditions," *Developmental Psychology* 26, no. 6 (1990): 978–86; Tyler R. Sasser, Karen L. Bierman, and Brenda Heinrichs, "Executive Functioning and School Adjustment: The Mediational Role of Pre-Kindergarten Learning-Related Behaviors," *Early Childhood Research Quarterly* 30, Pt. A (2015): 70–79.

3. Tanya R. Schlam et al., "Preschoolers' Delay of Gratification Predicts Their Body Mass 30 Years Later," *The Journal of Pediatrics* 162, no. 1 (January 2013): 90–93.

4. Megan M. McClelland et al., "Relations Between Preschool Attention Span-Persistence and Age 25 Education Outcomes," *Early Childhood Research Quarterly* 28, no. 2 (2013): 314–24.

5. Terrie E. Moffitt et al., "A Gradient of Childhood Self-Control Predicts Health, Wealth, and Public Safety," *Proceedings of the National Academy of Sciences of the United States of America* 108, no. 7 (2011): 2693–98.

6. Center on the Developing Child at Harvard University, *Enhancing and Practicing Executive Function Skills with Children from Infancy to Adolescence*, accessed May 31, 2017, developingchild.harvard.edu/resources/

activities-guide-enhancing-and-practicing-executive-function-skills-with-children-from-infancy-to-adolescence/.

7. Thomas E. Brown, "Inside the ADD Mind," *ADDitude Magazine*, April/May 2006, brownadhdclinic.com/wp-content/uploads/2013/05/additude-1.pdf.

8. Center on the Developing Child at Harvard University, "Building the Brain's 'Air Traffic Control' System: How Early Experiences Shape the Development of Executive Function (Working Paper No. 11)," accessed May 31, 2017, developingchild.harvard.edu/wp-content/uploads/2011/05/How-Early-Experiences-Shape-the-Development-of-Executive-Function.pdf; Adele Diamond, "Executive Functions," *Annual Review of Psychology* 64 (2013): 135–68.

9. Leah Savion, "Clinging to Discredited Beliefs: The Larger Cognitive Story," *Journal of the Scholarship of Teaching and Learning* 9, no. 1 (January 2009): 81–92.

10. Katherine M. Brown et al., *Investigative Case Management for Missing Children; Homicides: Report II* (Attorney General of Washington and U.S. Department of Justice Office of Juvenile Justice and Delinquency Prevention, 2006), accessed August 24, 2017, missingkids.com/en_US/archive/documents/homicide_missing.pdf; Alexia Cooper and Erica L. Smith, *Homicide Trends in the United States, 1980–2008: Annual Rates for 2009 and 2010* (U.S. Department of Justice, Bureau of Justice Statistics, November 2011: NCJ 236018), accessed May 31, 2017, bjs.gov/content/pub/pdf/htus8008.pdf; The Federal Bureau of Investigation, "NCIC Missing Person and Unidentified Person Statistics for 2014 Pursuant to Public Law 101-647, 104 Statute 4967, Crime Control Act of 1990 Requirements," accessed May 31, 2017, archives.fbi.gov/archives/about-us/cjis/ncic/ncic-missing-person-and-unidentified-person-statistics-for-2014#three.

11. Stephen P. Hinshaw and Richard M. Scheffler, *The ADHD Explosion: Myth, Medication, and Today's Push for Performance* (New York: Oxford University Press, 2014).

12. Dimitri A. Christakis et al., "Early Television Exposure and Subsequent Attentional Problems in Children," *Pediatrics* 113, no. 4 (April 2004): 708–13; Edward L. Swing et al., "Television and Video Game Exposure and the Development of Attention Problems," *Pediatrics* 126, no. 2 (June 2010): 214–21.

13. Alison Gopnik, Virginia Slaughter, and Andrew Meltzoff, "Changing Your Views: How Understanding Visual Perception Can Lead to a New Theory of Mind," in *Children's Early Understanding of Mind: Origins and Development*, eds. Charlie Lewis and Peter Mitchell (New York: Psychology Press, 1994), 157–81.

14. Adele Diamond et al., "Preschool Program Improves Cognitive Control," *Science* 318, no. 5855 (November 30, 2007): 1387–88.

15. Joseph A. Durlak et al., "The Impact of Enhancing Students' Social and Emotional Learning: A Meta-Analysis of School-Based Universal Interventions," *Child Development* 82, no. 1 (January/February 2011): 405–32. doi:10.1111/j.1467-8624.2010.01564.x.

16. Stephanie L. Haft, Chelsea A. Myers, and Fumiko Hoeft, "Socio-Emotional and Cognitive Resilience in Children with Reading Disabilities," *Current Opinion in Behavioral Sciences* 10 (August 2016): 133–41.

17. "What Research Says About the Value of Homework: Research Review," The Center for Public Education, accessed May 31, 2017, centerforpubliceducation.org/Main-Menu/Instruction/What-research-says-about-the-value-of-homework-At-a-glance/What-research-says-about-the-value-of-homework-Research-review.html.

18. Philip M. Sadler and Robert H. Tai, "Success in Introductory College Physics: The Role of High School Preparation," *Science Education* 85, no. 2 (2001): 111–36.

19. "Research Spotlight on Homework: NEA Reviews of the Research on Best Practices in Education," National Education Association, accessed May 31, 2017, nea.org/tools/16938.htm.

20. "Stress in America Findings," America Psychological Association, accessed May 31, 2017, apa.org/news/press/releases/stress/2010/national-report.pdf.

21. Jenny S. Radesky et al., "Parent Perspectives on Their Mobile Technology Use: The Excitement and Exhaustion of Parenting While Connected," *Journal of Developmental & Behavioral Pediatrics* 37, no. 9 (November/December 2016): 694–701.

Part 2. The A-E-I-O-U and Y of Childhood Well-Being

1. Frank J. Elgar, Wendy Craig, and Stephen J. Trites, "Family Dinners, Communication, and Mental Health in Canadian Adolescents,"*Journal of Adolescent Health* 52, no. 4 (April 2013): 433–38.

2. W. Steven Barnett et al., "Educational Effects of the Tools of the Mind Curriculum: A Randomized Trial," *Early Childhood Research Quarterly* 23, no. 3 (2008): 299–313.

3. Sheila Eyberg and Beverly Funderburk, *Parent-Child Interaction Therapy Protocol* (Gainesville, FL: PCIT International Publishing, 2011).

4. Center on the Developing Child at Harvard University, *Enhancing and Practicing Executive Function Skills with Children from Infancy to Adolescence*, accessed May 31, 2017, developingchild.harvard.edu/resources/activities-guide-enhancing-and-practicing-executive-function-skills-with-children-from-infancy-to-adolescence/.

5. Angeline S. Lillard and Jennifer Peterson, "The Immediate Impact of Different Types of Television on Young Children's Executive Function," *Pediatrics* 128, no. 4 (October 2011): 644–49.

6. Nick Bilton, "Steve Jobs Was a Low-Tech Parent," *The New York Times*, September 10, 2014.

7. National Sleep Foundation, "National Sleep Foundation 2014 Sleep in America Poll Finds Children Sleep Better When Parents Establish Rules, Limit Technology, and Set a Good Example," news release, March 3, 2014, sleepfoundation.org/

media-center/press-release/national-sleep-foundation-2014-sleep-america-poll-finds-children-sleep.

8. Yalda T. Uhls et al., "Five Days at Outdoor Education Camp Without Screens Improves Preteen Skills with Nonverbal Emotion Cues,"*Computers in Human Behavior* 39 (October 2014): 387–92.

9. Jenny S. Radesky et al., "Parent Perspectives on Their Mobile Technology Use: The Excitement and Exhaustion of Parenting While Connected," *Journal of Developmental & Behavioral Pediatrics* 37, no. 9 (November/December 2016): 694–701.

10. Jack P. Shonkoff et al., "The Lifelong Effects of Early Childhood Adversity and Toxic Stress" (technical report from the American Academy of Pediatrics), *Pediatrics* 129, no. 1 (January 2012): e232–e246; Marilyn J. Essex et al., "Epigenetic Vestiges of Early Developmental Adversity: Childhood Stress Exposure and DNA Methylation in Adolescence," *Child Development* 84, no. 1 (January 2013): 58–75; Torsten Klengel et al., "Allele-Specific FKBP5 DNA Demethylation Mediates Gene-Childhood Trauma Interactions," *Nature Neuroscience* 16, no. 1 (January 2013): 33–41.

11. Adam W. Hanley et al., "Washing Dishes to Wash the Dishes: Brief Instruction in an Informal Mindfulness Practice," *Mindfulness* 6, no. 5 (October 2015): 1095–103.

12. Jon Kabat-Zinn, "Mindfulness-Based Interventions in Context: Past, Present, and Future," *Clinical Psychology: Science and Practice* 10, no. 2 (June 2003): 144–56. doi:10.1093/clipsy/bpg016.

13. Giacomo Rizzolatti et al. "Premotor Cortex and the Recognition of Motor Actions," *Cognitive Brain Research* 3, no. 2 (March 1996): 131–41; Giacomo Rizzolatti and Laila Craighero, "The Mirror-Neuron System," *Annual Review of Neuroscience* 27 (2004): 169–92.

14. Victoria Horner and Andrew Whiten, "Causal Knowledge and Imitation/Emulation Switching in Chimpanzees (*Pan troglodytes*) and Children (*Homo sapiens*)," *Animal Cognition* 8, no. 3 (July 2005): 164–81.

15. Federal Trade Commission, "Lumosity to Pay $2 Million to Settle FTC Deceptive Advertising Charges for Its 'Brain Training' Program," news release, January 6, 2016, ftc.gov/news-events/press-releases/2016/01/lumosity-pay-2-million-settle-ftc-deceptive-advertising-charges; Tamar Lewin, "No Einstein in Your Crib? Get a Refund," *The New York Times*, October 23, 2009.

16. Alan L. Mendelsohn et al., "The Impact of a Clinic-Based Literacy Intervention on Language Development in Inner-City Preschool Children," *Pediatrics* 107, no. 1 (January 2001): 130–34.

17. A. Weisleder et al., "Promotion of Positive Parenting and Prevention of Socioemotional Disparities," *Pediatrics* 137, no. 2 (February 2016): e20153239; Anne C. Hargrave and Monique Sénéchal, "A Book Reading Intervention with Preschool Children Who Have Limited Vocabularies: The Benefits of Regular Reading and Dialogic Reading," *Early Childhood Research Quarterly* 15, no. 1 (2000): 75–90; Corrie Goldman, "This Is Your Brain on Jane Austen, and Stanford Researchers Are Taking Notes," *Stanford Report*, September 7, 2012, news.stanford.edu/news/2012/september/austen-reading-fmri-090712.html.

18. Sarah B. Miles and Deborah Stipek, "Contemporaneous and Longitudinal Associations Between Social Behavior and Literacy Achievement in a Sample of Low-Income Elementary School Children," *Child Development* 77, no. 1 (January/February 2006): 103–17.

19. Frederick J. Zimmerman, Dimitri A. Christakis, and Andrew N. Meltzoff, "Associations Between Media Viewing and Language Development in Children Under Age 2 Years," *The Journal of Pediatrics* 151, no. 4 (October 2007): 364–68.

20. "Class Size and Student Achievement: Research Review," Center for Public Education, accessed May 17, 2017, centerforpubliceducation.org/Main-Menu/Organizing-a-school/Class-size-and-student-achievement-At-a-glance/Class-size-and-student-achievement-Research-review.html.

21. Nigel Hastings and Joshua Schwieso, "Tasks and Tables: The Effects of Seating Arrangements on Task Engagement in Primary Classrooms," *Educational Research* 37, no. 3 (1995): 279–91.

22. Richard E. Clark, Paul A. Kirschner, and John Sweller, "Putting Students on the Path to Learning: The Case for Fully Guided Instruction,"*American Educator* 36, no. 1 (Spring 2012): 6–11.

23. Louisa Moats, *Whole-Language High Jinks: How to Tell When "Scientifically-Based Reading Instruction" Isn't* (Dayton, OH: Thomas B. Fordham Institute, 2007), accessed May 31, 2017, files.eric.ed.gov/fulltext/ED498005.pdf.

24. Carol Weitzman et al., "Promoting Optimal Development: Screening for Behavioral and Emotional Problems,"*Pediatrics* 135, no. 2 (February 2005): 384–95.

25. Joseph F. Hagan Jr., Judith S. Shaw, and Paula M. Duncan, eds. *Bright Futures: Guidelines for Health Supervision of Infants, Children, and Adolescents*, 4th ed. (Elk Grove Village, IL: American Academy of Pediatrics, 2017).

26. Stephen V. Farone et al., "The Worldwide Prevalence of ADHD: Is It an American Condition?" *World Psychiatry* 2, no. 2 (June 2003): 104–13.

27. Russell A. Barkley, ed. *Attention-Deficit/Hyperactive Disorder: A Handbook for Diagnosis and Treatment*, 4th ed. (New York: The Guilford Press, 2015), 588.

28. Jalees Rehman, "Accuracy of Medical Information on the Internet," *Scientific American* (blog), August 2, 2012, blogs.scientificamerican.com/guest-blog/accuracy-of-medical-information-on-the-internet/.

29. Daniel Willingham, "How Many People Believe Learning Styles Theories Are Right? And Why?" *Science & Education* (blog), September 4, 2017, danielwillingham.com/daniel-willingham-science-and-education-blog/how-many-people-believe-learning-styles-theories-are-right-and-why.

30. Alan G. Kamhi, "What Speech-Language Pathologists Need to Know About Auditory Processing Disorder," *Language, Speech, and Hearing Services in Schools* 42, no. 3 (July 2011): 265–72.

31. Marc E. Fey et al., "Auditory Processing Disorder and Auditory/Language Interventions: An Evidence-Based Systematic Review," *Language, Speech, and Hearing Services in Schools* 42, no. 3 (July 2011): 246–64.

32. American Academy of Pediatrics, "Sensory Integration Therapies for Children with Developmental and Behavioral Disorders" (policy statement, Section on Complementary and Integrative Medicine, Council on Children with Disabilities), *Pediatrics* 129, no. 6 (June 2012): 1186–89; American Academy of Pediatrics, Subcommittee on Attention-Deficit/Hyperactivity Disorder and Committee on Quality Improvement, "Clinical Practice Guideline: Treatment of the School-Aged Child with Attention-Deficit/Hyperactivity Disorder," *Pediatrics* 108, no. 4 (October 2001): 1033–44; Scott M. Myers and Chris Plauché Johnson, "Management of Children with Autism Spectrum Disorders," *Pediatrics* 120, no. 5 (November 2007): 1162–82.

33. "Vision Therapy," American Association for Pediatric Ophthalmology and Strabismus, accessed May 31, 2017, aapos.org/terms/conditions/108; American Academy of Pediatrics, Section on Ophthalmology et al., "Joint Statement—Learning Disabilities, Dyslexia, and Vision," *Pediatrics* 124, no. 2 (August 2009): 837–44.

34. "Autism and Vaccines," Autism Science Foundation, accessed September 28, 2017, autismsciencefoundation.org/what-is-autism/autism-and-vaccines; Margaret A. Maglione et al., "Safety of Vaccines Used for Routine Immunization of U.S. Children: A Systematic Review," *Pediatrics* 134, no. 2 (August 2014): 325–37; Luke E. Taylor, Amy L. Swerdfeger, and Guy D. Eslick, "Vaccines Are Not Associated with Autism: An Evidence-Based Meta-Analysis of Case-Control and Cohort Studies," *Vaccine* 32, no. 29 (June 17, 2014): 3623–29.

35. Claudia M. Mueller and Carol S. Dweck, "Praise for Intelligence Can Undermine Children's Motivation and Performance," *Journal of Personality and Social Psychology* 75, no. 1 (1998): 33–52.

36. Carol S. Dweck, *Mindset: The New Psychology of Success* (New York: Penguin Random House, 2006).

37. Angela L. Duckworth et al. "Grit: Perseverance and Passion for Long-Term Goals," *Journal of Personality and Social Psychology* 92, no. 6 (June 2007): 1087–101.

38. Christine Gross-Loh, "How Praise Became a Consolation Prize: Helping Children Confront Challenges Requires a More Nuanced Understanding of the 'Growth Mindset,'" *The Atlantic*, December 16, 2016, accessed May 31, 2017, theatlantic.com/education/archive/2016/12/how-praise-became-a-consolation-prize/510845/.

Part 3. Practical, Positive Parenting

1. Amy K. Drayton et al., "Internet Guidance on Time Out: Inaccuracies, Omissions, and What to Tell Parents Instead," *Journal of Developmental & Behavioral Pediatrics* 35, no. 4 (May 2014): 239–46.

2. Ibid.

3. Wendy Mogel, *The Blessing of a B Minus: Using Jewish Teachings to Raise Resilient Teenagers* (New York: Simon & Schuster, 2010).

4. Jeffrey Jensen Annett, "Emerging Adulthood: A Theory of Development from the Late Teens Through the Twenties," *American Psychologist* 55, no. 5 (2000): 469–80.

5. Madeline A. Dalton et al., "Use of Cigarettes and Alcohol by Preschoolers While Role-Playing as Adults: 'Honey, Have Some Smokes,'" *Archives of Pediatrics and Adolescent Medicine* 159 (2005): 854–59.

6. Madeline A. Dalton et al., "Child-Targeted Fast-Food Television Advertising Exposure Is Linked with Fast-Food Intake Among Pre-School Children," *Public Health Nutrition* 20, no. 9 (2017): 1–9, doi:10.1017/S1368980017000520; B. Sadeghirad et al., "Influence of Unhealthy Food and Beverage Marketing on Children's Dietary Intake and Preference: A Systematic Review and Meta-Analysis of Randomized Trials," *Obesity Reviews*

17, no. 10 (October 2016): 945–59, doi:10.1111/obr.12445; Emma J. Boyland et al., "Advertising as a Cue to Consume: A Systematic Review and Meta-Analysis of the Effects of Acute Exposure to Unhealthy Food and Nonalcoholic Beverage Advertising on Intake in Children and Adults," *American Journal of Clinical Nutrition* 103, no. 2 (2016): 519–33.

7. Lise Graversen et al., "Preschool Weight and Body Mass Index in Relation to Central Obesity and Metabolic Syndrome in Adulthood," *PLoS One* 9 (2014): e89986. doi:10.1371/journal. pone.0089986.

8. "How Children Learn to Like New Food," Ellyn Satter Institute, accessed May 18, 2017, ellynsatterinstitute.org/htf/ howchildrenlearntolikenewfood.php.

9. Cindy-Lee Dennis and Lori Ross, "Relationships Among Infant Sleep Patterns, Maternal Fatigue, and Development of Depressive Symptomatology," *Birth* 32 (2005): 187–93. doi:10.1111/j.0730-7659.2005.00368.x.

10. Michael Gradisar et al., "Behavioral Interventions for Infant Sleep Problems: A Randomized Controlled Trial," *Pediatrics* 137, no. 6 (2016): e20151486. doi:10.1542/peds.2015-1486.

11. Jodi A. Mindell et al., American Academy of Sleep Medicine, "Behavioral Treatment of Bedtime Problems and Night Wakings in Infants and Young Children," *Sleep* 29, no. 10 (2006): 1263–76.

12. Yvonne Kelly, John Kelly, and Amanda Sacker, "Time for Bed: Associations with Cognitive Performance in 7-Year-Old Children: A Longitudinal Population-Based Study," *Journal of Epidemiology and Community Health* 67, no. 11 (November 2013): 926–31.

13. Task Force on Sudden Infant Death Syndrome, "SIDS and Other Sleep-Related Infant Deaths: Updated 2016 Recommendations for a Safe Infant Sleeping Environment," *Pediatrics* 138 (2016), e20162938.

14. Heather L. Kirkorian et al., "The Impact of Background Television on Parent-Child Interaction," *Child Development* 80, no. 5 (September/October 2009): 1350–59.

15. Shalini Misra et al., "The iPhone Effect," *Environment and Behavior* 48, no. 2 (2014): 275–98.

16. Robert A. Emmons and Michael E. McCullough, "Counting Blessings Versus Burdens: An Experimental Investigation of Gratitude and Subjective Well-Being in Daily Life," *Journal of Personal and Social Psychology* 84, no. 2 (February 2003): 377–89.

Part 4. Mindfulness and Families

1. Matthew A. Killingsworth and Daniel T. Gilbert, "A Wandering Mind Is an Unhappy Mind," *Science* 330, no. 6006 (2010): 932.

2. Erik Wallmark et al., "Promoting Altruism Through Meditation: An 8-Week Randomized Controlled Pilot Study," *Mindfulness* 4, no. 3 (2013): 223–34.

3. Lori Haase et al., "When the Brain Does Not Adequately Feel the Body: Links Between Low Resilience and Interoception," *Biological Psychology* 113 (2016): 37–45.

4. Shwetha Nair et al., "Do Slumped and Upright Postures Affect Stress Response? A Randomized Trial," *Health Psychology* 34, no. 6 (2015): 632–41.

5. Typically attributed to psychologist and meditation instructor Tara Brach.

6. Todd B. Kashdan, Lisa Feldman Barrett, and Patrick E. McKnight, "Unpacking Emotion Differentiation: Transforming Unpleasant Experience by Perceiving Distinctions in Negativity," *Current Directions in Psychological Science* 24, no. 1 (2015): 10–16.

7. Remi Noguchi et al., "Effects of Five-Minute Internet-Based Cognitive Behavioral Therapy and Simplified Emotion-Focused Mindfulness on Depressive Symptoms: A Randomized Controlled Trial," *BMC Psychiatry* 17, no. 1 (2017): 85, doi:10.1186/s12888-017-1248-8.

8. Martin E. P. Seligman, "Building Resilience," *Harvard Business Review*, April 2011, accessed May 31, 2017, hbr.org/2011/04/building-resilience.

9. Pema Chödrön, *Practicing Peace in Times of War: A Buddhist Perspective* (Boston: Shambhala Publications, Inc., 2006).
10. Kristin D. Neff and Katie A. Dahm, "Self-Compassion: What It Is, What It Does, and How It Relates to Mindfulness," in *Mindfulness and Self-Regulation*, eds. M. Robinson, B. Meier, and B. Ostafin (New York: Springer, in press); Kayla Isaacs et al., "Psychological Resilience in U.S. Military Veterans: A 2-Year, Nationally Representative Prospective Cohort Study," *Journal of Psychiatric Research* 84 (2017): 301–09.
11. Lisa Flook et al., "Promoting Prosocial Behavior and Self-regulatory Skills in Preschool Children Through a Mindfulness-Based Kindness Curriculum," *Developmental Psychology* 51, no. 1 (2015): 44–51; Daniel Lim, Paul Condon, and David DeSteno, "Mindfulness and Compassion: An Examination of Mechanism and Scalability," *PLoS One* 10, no. 2 (2015): e0118221; Antoine Lutz et al., "Regulation of the Neural Circuitry of Emotion by Compassion Meditation: Effects of Meditative Expertise," *PLoS One* 3, no. 3 (2008): e1897.

About the Author

MARK BERTIN, MD, is a developmental pediatrician in Pleasantville, New York. He attended the UCLA School of Medicine, trained in general pediatrics at Oakland Children's Hospital, and later completed fellowship training in neurodevelopmental behavioral pediatrics at the Albert Einstein College of Medicine. Dr. Bertin is the author of *Mindful Parenting for ADHD* and *The Family ADHD Solution*, which integrate mindfulness with other evidence-based ADHD care, and he is a contributing author for the book *Teaching Mindfulness Skills to Kids and Teens*.

Dr. Bertin is a faculty member at New York Medical College and the Windward Teacher Training Institute, and he is on the advisory boards for the nonprofit organizations Common Sense Media and Reach Out and Read. His blog is available through *Huffington Post*, Mindful.org, and *Psychology Today*. Dr. Bertin also leads mindfulness classes, often for groups of parents or physicians. For more information, please visit his website at developmentaldoctor.com.

About Sounds True

SOUNDS TRUE is a multimedia publisher whose mission is to inspire and support personal transformation and spiritual awakening. Founded in 1985 and located in Boulder, Colorado, we work with many of the leading spiritual teachers, thinkers, healers, and visionary artists of our time. We strive with every title to preserve the essential "living wisdom" of the author or artist. It is our goal to create products that not only provide information to a reader or listener, but that also embody the quality of a wisdom transmission.

For those seeking genuine transformation, Sounds True is your trusted partner. At SoundsTrue.com you will find a wealth of free resources to support your journey, including exclusive weekly audio interviews, free downloads, interactive learning tools, and other special savings on all our titles.

To learn more, please visit SoundsTrue.com/freegifts or call us toll-free at 800.333.9185.

sounds True
many voices, one journey